WHY AREN'T YOU SUCCESSFUL? ...YET

FROM SOMEONE WHO ASKED HIMSELF THE SAME QUESTION

ODUDU 'EMMILLIO' INYANG

WHY AREN'T YOU SUCCESSFUL?... YET
Copyright © 2022 by Odudu 'Emmillio' Inyang

Paper Back ISBN: 978-1-7396646-1-9
Hardback ISBN: 978-1-7396646-2-6
Ebook ISBN: 978-1-7396646-0-2

DEDICATION

This book is dedicated to...

Every single person who has ever asked themself the title question
(or any variation of it).

Every person who has felt that success was never meant for them

Every person who has ever had issues felt good enough

Every person who has been or continues to be scared to be themselves

Every person who has at some point been so hurt by life
that they choose to not let anyone in

Every person who has been told that they are successful,
but feel like something is missing.

And finally, I dedicate this book to the past and future versions of myself.

You are all the reasons why this book exists.
And just as you have all helped me, I pray this book helps you. #

CONTENTS

- 0.0 -
PROLOGUE:
WHO AM I (BEFORE WRITING THIS BOOK)

"I am a self employed audio engineer, music producer and music tutor. With that being said, I wouldn't say I'm successful (not in the least) and I'm frustrated as to why. As of writing this, I'm 30 years old and thought that I would be successful a whole lot sooner. This is magnified by the fact that I am blessed to have friends around me that are what I consider to be successful (many of which I've actually helped get to that point), which led me to ask myself the question of why I'm not successful yet. Many of these same people would seek my counsel and pick my brain on what they could and should be doing in their own lives. I've known what I've wanted to do for some time and yet I don't feel like I've made the inroads that I should have by now. They say that to know is to do and I simply haven't been doing enough of the things that I know I need to do, to be successful. Finally, I'm at a place in my life where I don't feel like I have much to show for my efforts, in comparison to those around me"

- 0.5 -
INTRODUCTION:
THE GOAL OF THIS BOOK AND HOW TO USE IT

I've always loved reading, especially self help books and have always wanted to write one. I truly love helping others and have been told numerous times by numerous people that I should be a motivational speaker/life-coach/teacher/author/consultant/etc. I've also been asked many times "When are you writing a book?" which would always make me laugh. But it's something I've always wanted to do.

That being said, I didn't want to be one of those who earned a living from telling people to do things that I've never done, or write a book that I wasn't qualified to write. But rather than let that stop me from achieving a dream and writing a book, I asked myself:

"If I had to write a book today and it could only be based on what I know right now, what would it be called and what would it be based on?"

And that's how this book was conceived. As much as I love self improvement and motivational books, reading them would only make me *'feel'* better, when I wanted to *'become'* better. Reading books alone just makes you sound like you know what you're talking about. It doesn't necessarily mean you've applied the information you regurgitate in conversation.

I have two goals for this book, a selfish one and a selfless one. If I was writing this book just 'to help people', I'd be lying to you and I feel that 90% of people who say that are also lying. The selfish goal of this book is for me to look within myself to identify the reasons why I don't feel I'm successful....yet, whilst documenting my journey on becoming successful.

The more selfless goal of this book is simple; *"To 'inspire' you on **your own** journey to success, by **openly sharing with you** my own."*

Let's be clear on a few things. I define and measure 'inspire' by the following

- The actions YOU TAKE
- The person YOU BECOME
- NOT simply how YOU FEEL

This book would have truly failed its purpose if it made you feel good, but you didn't notice any real changes within yourself. From life experience, I've learned that people often learn more from what they see others do, than what they are told from them. An example of this is with children. Often children mimic the behaviour they see from people they admire (e.g., family, friends, etc) instead of mimicking what those same people tell them to do. In an African household for example, it isn't uncommon to have heard "Do as I Say, Not as I Do"

HOW TO USE THIS BOOK

The simple answer to this question is...

"Whatever works best for you"

The reason why this is the case is simply because I want you to understand that there is more than one way of achieving a positive outcome and to not be fixated on doing I say this because I want you to understand that there is more than one way of achieving a positive outcome and to not be fixated on doing something a particular way (that itself is a mistake that I've been constantly making)

I've organised this book into sections, named after each reason why I don't feel that I'm successful...yet. Each section is designed to share my story on discovering the reason but also share my journey to addressing them.

You can look at the contents page and start with the reason that you resonate with the most and read from that part onwards. In each section I share my truth relating to it, the principles that I learned addressing it and my toolbox of tasks/activities that helped me address those reasons (which may also help you).

These tasks and activities are outlined in the companion workbook. Prompts to each exercise are mentioned at the best time to do them (with workbook page numbers included e.g. WB PG___). This was important to me, as the books I got the most value from were those that gave practical opportunities throughout the book for the reader to apply the information that was provided.

NB: If you are more fascinated with my journey, then just keep reading and skip the exercises/challenges (that being said, you may gain more value from trying them out).

If I were to make one recommendation, it would be to read Reason Zero first. This is because you may read this section alone and realise that you are already successful and thus end up having a better outlook on life (that would mean the world to me if anyone contacted me saying that).

FOR ALL OF THOSE WHO ALSO LOVE SELF IMPROVEMENT BOOKS

If there is one value that I discovered and try to live by that I want to bestow upon you before we start, it would be this....

VALUE #1: TO WIN IS TO TRY

This book is FAR more about trying than talking or even reading, which is why not only is each chapter filled with exercises, I want to focus on spending 5 mins on each one (unless you finish it sooner). I don't want you to look at any of the exercises and feel like you're not ready to try them, or you have to take your time with them. Over thinking things (especially in my case) is what can delay and even stall your chances of being successful. All of these exercises I've personally tried (and done), as I don't believe in asking others to try/do something I wouldn't myself.

NB: Have you noticed how common it can be to define yourself by what you have done and haven't <u>done</u>, compared to what you have and haven't <u>tried?</u>

I want you to feel like you've won just by trying. This will be discussed later on in the book

The goal of each exercise is to get them started. You can finish them in your own time if you don't finish them within the deadline. If you are struggling with finishing any of the exercises I suggest you label It: Exercise "insert number here" (1st Draft). This is important because the more you try and make things perfect, the more time you may spend procrastinating and hesitating. That being said, I've designed them to make it practical and simple enough to do, regardless of your circumstances.

The most important part of this whole journey is for you to routinely make time to pursue success, and everyone has to start somewhere.

This book is about changing the perception of success from a destination, into a journey with many stops (milestones). I hope you enjoy reading this and watching me go on my journey inspires you to go on your own. Let's get started ....

REASON ZERO:
I DIDN'T DISCOVER AND/OR ACCEPT MY DEFINITION OF SUCCESS SOONER

SIGNS & SYMPTOMS THAT YOU ARE SUFFERING FROM THIS INCLUDE, BUT ARE NOT LIMITED TO;

1. Confusion/lack of clarity
2. Caring too much what other people think
3. Lacking focus
4. Caring too much about material things (e.g. money, fame)
5. Seeking the approval of others, rather than yourself (people pleasing)
6. Defining yourself by your weaknesses

OBJECTIVE(S):

1. To discover one's definition of success
2. To accept one's definition of success
3. To assess how close or far away one is from achieving their definition of success
4. To discover strategies to help bridge the gap (if necessary)

My Truth

"As I child, not only did I want to be successful, but I was obsessed with the idea of being successful at a young age (before 25). I almost felt like being successful at a young age was the only way to validate myself, as I felt anyone could be successful by the time they were old (at that time, being 30+ was old to me). I was always fixated on being able to do things that no one else could do. Maybe because I wanted to prove to the world how special I was. I defined success by money. I wanted to be a millionaire and have a ton of plaques on the wall from all my achievements in the music industry. Success to me was very much based on impressing others and showing off how special I felt I was.

Success to me now though is something different. Success to me is being able to earn more money than I need from doing the things I enjoy but also having the time to live the life that I want to live. What kind of life is that you ask? I have a whole bucket list for that but I am someone who prefers experiences.

I've always wanted to go on a hot air balloon for example, I have a long list of countries I've always wanted to go to (Cuba, Brazil, Paris, Egypt, Dominican Republic, Trinidad, etc)

Success to me is also being the man who personifies who I would want any of my (future) sons to be like, whilst also having a wife who is a walking example of who I would want any of my (future) daughter(s) to be like. Settling down and raising children to not only gain financial freedom from their own passions but to positively contribute to the world.

Which leads me to my last thought. Success to me is leaving a legacy; a legacy of projects/missions that bring value to the world and can run without me, but also a legacy of people that I've helped along their journey and are bringing real value to the world.

I will admit though, and this is selfish of me to say, I want to be Remembered. Not famous I might add, but Remembered."

- 01 -
WHAT IS SUCCESS TO YOU?

"Success is walking from failure to failure with no loss of enthusiasm."
Winston Churchill

According to the Oxford Dictionary, successful has two definitions…

Adjective
1. Accomplishing a desired aim or result
2. Having achieved fame, wealth or social status

This was the second question I asked myself at the start of this journey. The first one was "Am I Successful?" (as documented in my truth). It's good to have an idea of where you think you are and what you think success is to you currently to see if your answers will change when you finish this book.

NB: You will have to continue reading to see if my answers changed from the beginning to the end of the journey.

EXERCISE #0: PRE QUESTIONNAIRE (WB PG 6)

Many of us have our own ideas of what success is, whether we use that definition to judge others or ourselves. I would argue however that one of the biggest reasons why people aren't successful is because they've allowed their understanding of it to be shaped by other influences. These include, but aren't limited to;

- Friends
- Family
- Life experience(s)
- Culture
- Religion
- Media (E.g. Magazines, Social Media)
- People that impress you
- People you want to impress

WHY IS MY DEFINITION OF SUCCESS IMPORTANT?

I realised that it was important to establish my definition of success for a multitude of reasons. One being that the clearer I am in my definition of success in a particular situation, the more likely I was to achieve it. Additionally I realised that I was happier to do what was necessary to increase my chances of achieving success.

Another big reason why this is important is because it will make the 'difficult' choices you are going to have to make, not as difficult. There will be many people who will try to impose their definition of success on you, as well as those who will attempt to make you feel doubt in your own sense of success. Mostly this won't be due to malice, but more about their own beliefs. Whenever this would happen to me I felt that this was the universe's way of telling me that I was wrong and I would try to learn (almost as if I was only ever right if someone else told me). What I've realised is that whilst it's important to be open to learning from others, it's also important to develop a foundation that you are prepared to stand up for; against any and all opposition.

WHAT IF (INSERT DEITY YOU BELIEVE IN HERE) AND/OR THE UNIVERSE ONLY TOLD YOU THE TRUTH ABOUT YOU?"...

17

I started asking myself this question. This came from reflecting on many situations I found myself in, both professionally and personally. A common situation would be where I had an instinct on what would happen and on the action that should be taken, I would then be told by someone else another action that should be take and I would allow myself to defer to them (because of how convinced-of-themselves they seemed, even though I thought they were wrong). The situation would then go exactly the way I thought it would go.

To provide a deeper background on this; as a kid I was always what I would consider 'politely stubborn'. It's probably why I could always relate to troublesome kids. Whatever I believed, it was nigh on impossible to convince me otherwise. I could think the sky was purple and nobody could convince me otherwise. The only way I learnt was from experience. The only difference between myself and some of the other troublesome kids growing up was that I was polite enough to make others in authority think I'm listening to them and keeping my thoughts to myself, rather than openly disagreeing. I then began compartmentalising that stubborn part of myself and ended up simply deferring to others. That stubborn part of me however was still there.

If you've ever been stubborn yourself and know anyone stubborn, you'll know that the only way that stubborn people learn is through experience. Many of us have to get our fingers burned to realise not to play with fire. My stubbornness didn't necessarily come from not believing people...

IT CAME FROM THE BELIEF THAT BECAUSE OF HOW 'GIFTED' I AM, MANY OF WHAT IS TRUE FOR OTHERS, WON'T APPLY TO ME

If a teacher would tell me in the classroom that I would need to revise say 10 hours a week for school, I would feel "That's for everyone else, I can get away with doing it in less".

I got the balance wrong between following my instincts and being open to learning. I truly believe that seeking clarity in my definition of success would have made it easier to make the balance

So how do I discover my definition of success?

What helped me discover my definition of success was when I began seeing success as a journey, with many milestones/pit stops, instead of a single destination. This means that you can start the journey without being too sure of where the destination is.

For too long I also felt that there was only one route towards success, and if I wasn't following that one route, I was a failure. The greatest thing about a journey is that it doesn't have to end at one destination.. You can add different milestones/pit stops, you can go in different directions and even take different routes, because the journey is more important than the destination.

So with shifting my perspective, I asked myself...

"So what milestones would I want to experience/
accomplish before I die?"...

One of the ways you can do this is by writing a bucket list. For those of you that don't know what it is, a bucket list is...

"a number of experiences or achievements that a person
hopes to have or accomplish during their lifetime"

DON'T DEFINE SUCCESS SOLELY ON THE THINGS YOU HAVEN'T ACCOMPLISHED, AS YOU MAY HAVE ALREADY ACCOMPLISHED SOME LEVEL OF SUCCESS

The most vital part of doing a bucket list is that you write the things you've always wanted to do, as well as the things that you <u>have already done</u> . This is vital to giving you perspective on where you REALLY are, instead of where you FEEL you are.

On to the next exercise. You'll also find some guide questions in the workbook for this one and the reason why is because you may find there are multiple layers to your definition of success.....

NB: See this exercise as fun, rather than daunting.

EXERCISE #1: BUCKET LIST (WB PG 7)

Looking back at your lists, how do you feel? Do you feel like 5 minutes was enough time?

The reason why I set the deadline so short is because this exercise is simply about you making a start on the journey. It doesn't have to be perfect and it doesn't have to be finished at this stage, it just has to be honest to you, and when you are being honest with yourself, it shouldn't take as long to come up with answers (compared to if you're trying to live for others).

This exercise is also about jump-starting your mind into thinking this way. A bucket list isn't something you should do just once, it should be something that you constantly look at and tweak as and when necessary. This will naturally happen. By going on this journey, you will discover that your definition of success has many layers. These layers will often be discovered by your experiences, your personal reflection of those experiences and how you reacted to them.

To take too long starting a bucket list robs you of the time you can spend on the journey. Imagine taking 10 hours to plan a journey that could take 30 mins if you just started walking now. It's an extreme example I know, but it illustrates the point that whilst planning is important, it shouldn't get in the way of you actually living life.

I didn't realise this until much later but my definition of success is a liquid concept, in the sense that I accept that I may discover more layers to it just by going on this journey. Your definition of success is like your compass that allows you to decide which direction to go in, what choices to make and how to navigate the 'terrain'.

- 02 -
THE TERRAIN 101: WHAT IS IT?

"The best way to get people to venture into unknown terrain is to make it desirable by taking them there in their imaginations"

Noel Tichy

Terrain: *noun*

1. a stretch of land, especially with regard to its physical features. "they were delayed by rough terrain"

Imagine being stranded in a large forest and it is dark. You can't see any signs of civilization in any direction. You can barely see in front of your own hands, but you can see numerous signs with directions to different places and there are animals, insects and plants around, but you don't know which ones can help you or hurt you. And just to make it more of a challenge, it starts raining, making the ground muddy

Put simply, the terrain is **<u>your environment</u>**. There are so many more options out there in life now than there ever was in previous generations and as a result the environment has become more clustered, thus more difficult to navigate. I feel that many of the previous generations' attitude was based on 'You make your bed, you lie in it', whereby they would feel like they have to stand by the choices they made in perpetuity. By comparison, in this generation you can abandon ship and change your mind anytime you want (a great example of this is the modern divorce rate numbers compared to that in the 1950s and earlier). People now have more options and more choices. When I was growing up there were only four channels on TV and the idea of Channel 5 was mind blowing. Now there are countless TV channels, never mind the fact that you can watch TV on the internet or via your smartphone. In today's times, I would say the most challenging elements of one's terrain to navigate are the abundance of information, tools, people and situations.

NB: This specifically applies more to the western world and more developed countries than other parts of the world (such as impoverished nations - I hate saying third world).

To be more specific, I'll include a list for each element. None of the following lists are exhaustive (as I would argue books can be written on each one alone), it is simply there to give you an insight into each element of the terrain.

<u>Information</u>

Following the analogy mentioned at the beginning of this chapter, information is the numerous signs and directions to different places in the dark forest. They pretty much serve to answer one or more of the following questions

- What...
- Who...
- Why
- When...
- Where...
- How..

This is otherwise known as 5W1H and the foundation behind information, Information once upon a time was more difficult to access than it is now. When I was growing up, information was found via books and encyclopedias.

You first had to even know that the book existed and from there you had to find the place where it was. The best location were libraries as many of these books were expensive and beyond people's means. Also known as reference books, they were of such value that libraries wouldn't even allow people take it out of the premises.

Now you can access the same information that millionaires used to build their wealth, all in minutes. You can pretty much find all the information you would need to get started via the internet. The challenge with the abundance of information is...

"Is the information correct?"
"What information should I apply?"
"How do I know that this will work for me?"

People
People are the animals, insects and plants in this analogy of the terrain. Some can help you, others can hurt you. This is true in a similar fashion to certain animals being edible and some insects or plants being poisonous. A non exhaustive list of the types of people include:

- People who aren't 'successful'
- People who tried but gave up on becoming 'successful'
- People who haven't discovered/accepted their true definition of success, and are trying to pursue someone else's'
- People who feel like their definition of success is more valid than yours
- People who you consider to be successful
- People who consider themselves to be successful
- People who are happy to help you become successful...

- People who are also striving to discover and pursue their definition of success
- People who you seek the approval of

I could go on forever with the list of people, but we will touch on that further in Reason 3. What's important is that you get an understanding for the fact that there are people that can make your journey easier, and there are people who can make your journey more difficult.

Situations

Situations are the weather in the forest.

- The Past & Your memories/interpretations of past situations
- The Present & Your perception/reaction of the present situation(s)
- The Future & Your forecast of the future situation(s)

As you can see with these lists; there are so many roads that you can go down that you can literally end up lost. You can get lost on your own, or you can get lost by following someone else's direction, that's the challenge.

I truly believe that if you deal with these three well, you can create an abundance of options and opportunities (both of which are also a challenge to navigate). If you don't deal with these things well, you can create and indulge in an abundance of distractions. I would go as far as to argue that your mind will often present distractions as a way of helping you escape the truth that you are not navigating the terrain well enough.

YOU WILL ALWAYS BE PRESENTED WITH A CHOICE, ITS FOR YOU TO BE AWARE WHENEVER YOU HAVE ONE, AND DISCOVER WHAT OPTION(S) WILL BEST HELP YOU

Having a better understanding of what success is to you can give you a clearer idea of how close (or far away) you are to it. But most importantly it makes it easier for you to deal with the terrain (especially if you discover that success is closer to you than you originally thought). I had to learn to realise that not every single person's definition of success is EXACTLY the same, so how could I expect my journey to be the same as everyone else's'?

Thinking about this I have to be honest and say I navigated the terrain terribly and one of the biggest reasons why is because I didn't even realise I was even in the terrain, never mind being aware of all the elements. I would often confuse information with knowledge and thus thought I knew more than I actually did.

In regards to people, I've been so easily swayed by others that I've often felt irritated at following their definition of success and seeing them happy, whilst I didn't. In regards to situations? I would mentally use my past situations as an excuse, almost as if those situations would condemn me forever to a life of unhappiness.

Regarding the terrain, just realising that there is one helped me and should help you realise that there will be obstacles to you achieving what you want to. But what I realised is that the terrain plays a prevalent role in all five of the reasons why I don't feel like I'm successful... yet. That being said, can discovering one's definition of success end at just writing a bucket list? Not quite.

- 03 -

PRIORITY MANAGEMENT 101: DISCOVERY (PART 1)

"The key is not to prioritise what's on your schedule, but to schedule your priorities"

Stephen Covey

When I first started exploring bucket lists, I got carried away and almost had bucket lists for everything. It was unfocused and I often ended up spending too much time on things that weren't as important to me (or weren't truly important at all).

I could write a whole book on prioritising and how much of a struggle it has been. The most difficult situation I would face would be when I felt like I had numerous priorities that were just as important as each other (in my opinion anyway). This would result in me feeling overwhelmed and thus deciding not to do anything. I also struggled with the concept of priorities because there were home truths about life that I didn't want to accept. A few of those truths are...

1) YOU HAVE NO REAL IDEA OF HOW MUCH TIME YOU HAVE BEFORE YOU DIE (AND YES YOU WILL DIE ONE DAY)

2) YOU PROBABLY WON'T GET TO ACCOMPLISH EVERYTHING YOU EVER WANTED TO IN YOUR LIFE

3) YOU MAY SPEND TOO MUCH OF YOUR TIME ON THINGS THAT JUST WEREN'T THAT IMPORTANT TO YOU

These truths can hit people differently and realising this brought up more internal issues than it addressed, which caused me to procrastinate on going on this journey. These were

1. Fear of dying/taking risks (discussed in Reason 2)
2. Fear of being exposed as not good enough (discussed in Reason 1)
3. Fear of getting my priorities wrong and wasting time (which can lead to doing nothing- and can even lead to you focusing on other people's priorities)

What scares me most about death is not achieving my true definition of success before I go. If you focus most of your time on the things that are most important to you, you should feel more 'successful'. It is easy to feel pressure to always make the right choice. However, what happens if you don't know whether you are making the right choice or not? Whilst asking myself this question, over time I realised...

YOU WILL OFTEN HAVE TO MAKE CHOICES IN MOMENTS WHERE YOU WON'T HAVE ALL THE INFORMATION, AND THIS IS SOMETHING YOU HAVE TO BE OK WITH

This is where I have to remind you (and myself) of the first principle I mentioned in the book; to win is to try. If you study people who you and/or society would consider successful; one of the things you may notice is that they habitually took the decision to try something, when they may not have been in the perfect circumstances to do so. Whether it was because others around them didn't think they were 'ready' (which is a very relative concept by the way) or the timing not being 'right'.

So to go back to the point, even though I'm going to share with you ideas of how I got better at prioritising, you have to realise that life experiences will shape and *reshape* your priorities, so accept the fact that not only can it change, but change(s) in this example can be a good thing.

Now, it's time to arrange one's Bucket List in order of priority (provided you did the exercise earlier in the book). This is important, because prioritising gives you a clearer idea of what success is to YOU. From doing this, you may even realise that you've been spending more of your time on things that you don't consider as much of a priority as you do with others.

"But what If I'm going to complete everything on my bucket list. Would it then not matter the order I do it in?"

This is a thought that would go through my head whenever I would think about prioritising. However, the reality is that knowing your priorities DOES matter. If you have ever read Rich Dad, Poor Dad by Robert Kiyosaki (which I strongly recommend by the way), one of the things it talks about is how poor people think...

'Do I go for option A OR B?'

whereas rich people think...

'How can I get BOTH A & B?'.

So, with that being said, how do we arrange our list to be more effective, but without entertaining the thought that we can't/won't achieve everything? You can do that by answering the following guidance questions.

"Let's say that you will achieve every item that is on your bucket list, what item would you want to achieve first?"

Asking yourself this question is important, because when you answer this, you may realise for example that Item #1 on your list is more important than Item #2, #3, and #4 combined.

"What item(s) on your bucket list scares you the most?"

The reason why this question is important is because the goals that you are most scared of are often the ones that you care about the most (for me especially)

"What item(s) on your bucket list fills you with the most happiness/fulfilment at the idea of achieving?"

Rather than learning to make constructive decisions based on just negative emotions, it's also important to not forget to factor in positive emotions. Don't worry if there are things that you are not sure about, you can always change them at any time as and when it suits you.

"What item(s) on the bucket list will bring you the most value?"

This one is an extension of the previous question. Similar to the fact that there are different types/definitions of success, there are also different types of value e.g. financial, emotional, etc.

"What item(s) on the bucket list can you achieve quickly?"

This final question is critical, because you may realise that a lot of the goals that answer the previous questions may take a significantly long time to achieve. If something takes too long to achieve it can often be more difficult to maintain the willpower to see it through to the end. What has often worked for me is when I have accomplished smaller wins on my way to the bigger win.

I also noticed that when tackling a bigger goal in my life I would neglect all the other goals that I have in mind. This created many toxic moments where my sense of happiness was reliant on one big goal that was going to take time regardless of how hard I worked at it. These situations would also mould my belief that my sense of happiness should be suspended until I achieved this one lofty goal. And that was a mistake. Happiness should be the state of mind and emotion you feel in the present moment, instead of only feeling it if you achieve a certain outcome.

EXERCISE #2: BUCKET LIST QUESTIONNAIRE (WB PG 9)

One of the negative patterns of behaviour I've noticed in myself is my impatience. I have a lot of goals I want to accomplish, and I want to achieve all of them at nearly the same time. As a result, this dramatically reduces my chances and most often leads me to not achieving anything.

I've been at my most effective when I've focused and simplified my goals in steps, rather than huge leaps. As you went through this exercise, you may have also noticed some items that can help you achieve others (e.g. your bucket list goal of owning your own business can very easily help you with your goal of visiting a foreign country).

Knowing which items are more important to YOU is valuable because it can influence your strategy. That being said, don't worry too much about a strategy for now. Another thing I noticed about doing this exercise is that the tasks that I feel would bring the most value to me were also the ones that I was most scared of and don't actually feel like doing. It also made it easier for me to understand why I have spent a lot of my life procrastinating.

With all that being said, I don't want you to feel pressured into pursuing your definition of success in a linear fashion. Doing so would lead to frustration, as life simply isn't linear and the more you can accept that, the better your life will be. It would be amazing if we could pursue our goals in the exact order of priority (like prioritising our goals isn't hard enough) but the reality is we could get stuck. From us not feeling we can do it right now, to the fact we actually might not be able to do it right now (e.g. I can't go to Brazil if I don't have a valid passport or visa). This is what led to the final question. Just because you can't tick off an item straight away, doesn't mean you can't work on the others instead. You may even find that a lower priority item may help you with the ones higher up on the list. What matters the most with this is that you are now working on things that mean something to you PERIOD. The order is just a general guideline.

Why? - One of Life's Greatest Questions

Asking yourself 'why?' as many times as possible in this context (and in life) can you give you a deeper understanding of what your definition of success is. In asking yourself this question you may even realise that what you thought you wanted isn't actually what you wanted. Asking this question of others will also help you empathise with them and improve your levels of compassion and understanding

Sidenote: You may end up having more than one bucket list. And this is *__perfectly fine__*. I actually encourage it and I myself have many, including but not limited to.

> Film/TV list: All the films I want to watch
> Music List: All the songs/albums I need to listen
> Book List: All the books I want to make time to read

Take your time with this though, but if/when you feel the urge, just do it.

FROM DEFINITION TO VISION

"Vision without action is merely a dream. Action without vision just passes the time. Vision with action can change the world"

Joel A. Barker

I soon realised that my definition of success involved being a leader. As a child I could always remember having issues with authority and taking orders. I would always say to myself that I was a leader, but I had to learn how to be a good one.

One thing this process of introspection has led me to is realising that leadership is not a logical process, but more emotional. To lead others to follow you has nothing to do with logic. I have made this mistake on many occasions where I have tried and failed to convince others to follow my lead by using logic and covertly implying how smart I was. I say this because a definition is logical, whereas vision is emotional. To further add to this point I realised that I wouldn't be able to achieve what I wanted in life without developing a vision and being able to sell that vision to others who could help.

The clearer that vision is to yourself, the easier it is to sell. People are drawn to those who have a clear vision of where they want to go and the more you are excited about the vision, the more likely they are to want to help.

At this stage the purpose of turning your definition into a vision is so that it helps fuel your motivation. Having a clear vision can make it easier to overcome the obstacles you will undoubtedly go through (otherwise known as navigating the terrain)

The things you may struggle with but need to accept are:

1. This is what you **actually** want (and if it isn't, this will help you get closer to discovering what you actually want)
2. It's **actually possible** to achieve
3. It's actually possible for **YOU** to achieve

Now that you have a bucket list (which for me was the first step) it is time to make it as real as possible in your mind. This is because the bucket list alone might be daunting to you and you may be tempted to dismiss it out of hand, or feel that you are not ready to go for it.

So how do I do this? There is always more than one way to an end goal, but I'll suggest to you two things that I tried.

1. A Vision Board - a board of pictures of the items on your bucket list you wish to accomplish.
2. A Bucket List Menu - a list of the items of your bucket list and how much it would cost to achieve.

THE MORE YOU COMMIT TO THE JOURNEY, THE MORE YOUR TRUE DEFINITION OF SUCCESS WILL REVEAL ITSELF TO YOU IN ALL OF ITS LAYERS

VISION BOARDS: ARE THEY WORTH MY TIME?

I have always been a dreamer, so much so that I wouldn't get anything done. As you can then imagine, when I first heard that I should visualise my success I dismissed it out of hand.

But then I watched the Secret. This was a film adapted from the well-known book of the same name, which is often credited for being the first book (definitely the most creative) to explain the Law of Attraction. For those of you who don't know, the Law of Attraction is a universal law that suggests that whatever we focus on is what we will attract.

From watching this film, I started trying to be more focused on the things I fantasised about. I watched The Secret at a time when I was transitioning from being on benefits (some of the best times of my life, but I'll mention that more in another book) to working and no longer needing to rely on the state to pay my bills.

Taking heed from the Secret, I would sit down and imagine in as much detail as I could, accomplishing a goal (at the time it was to own a car). So, I would imagine the smell of the inside of the car, the feeling of the steering wheel on my hands, the music that I would have playing. I would set a limit of 5mins (otherwise I'd be dreaming all day). After watching the film and practicing some of the things it suggested, I realised I became a lot more focused, but more importantly I became a lot more resilient. During this time, I was still doing studio sessions once a week, but I was now also working part time as a door-to-door charity fundraiser, where I could earn more money in the form of bonuses the better I did. For anyone who has ever done this or face to face sales, you will know how difficult it can be. Times can get tough, the weather can be brutal and the constant rejection can make you question your sanity. That being said I noticed that having the vision of owning the car during the tough moments of the job made it a lot easier to go through the rejection and the other pitfalls of the job.

The reason? It was because all of what I was going through felt like a fair trade for the vision that I had built up in my head. It also made me realise that the mind is prepared to endure a lot if it feels that the potential pay off is not only possible, but worth it. When other people around me were giving up or losing their cool due to the constant rejection (which is commonplace in fundraising and sales), I would bounce from door to door and visualising myself owning a car was the key to that. A few months later I had saved up enough money to buy the car that I was looking for. It felt amazing.

Then I found out about vision boards. As previously stated, when I first heard about vision boards I thought it was naff and something that only the elderly did. And then I actually tried it.

There are many articles and videos on youtube that can show you how to put together a vision (done by those far more qualified than myself. I would say, the act of making the vision board was more beneficial than the vision board itself was. That being said, what helped the most for me was having a photo album on my phone of all images that I saved. The most important part of doing this is to make time every single day to look at it so that you remember what your goals are.

From discovering this as one of the reasons why I feel I'm not success-ful...yet, I realised that I wouldn't look at my goals anywhere near often enough. I would look at it at the beginning of the year, on my birthday, and on the last day of the year. I've learned to realise that your goals are some-thing that you should make time to remind yourself of every day and that a vision board is a great way of making it feel real, rather than just reading words off a page/screen.

EXERCISE #3 VISION BOARD [WB PG 11]

The reason I wanted you to go and look for images of your definition of success is so that it will be easier for you to visualise your success. For ex-ample, part of your definition of success may be to go to Egypt on holiday, but you may not even know what Egypt looks like (Its landmarks, wildlife, most attractive city, cuisine, etc). The more you can visualise your definition of success, the more real it will feel and the easier you can navigate the terrain. It's always easier making your way out of a dark tunnel when you can visualise the light at the end of it.

BUCKET LIST MENU: HOW MUCH DOES THE DREAM COST?

I cannot recommend doing this highly enough. This is even more impactful because I, like many, had been conditioned to feel that I had to wait before I achieved certain elements of my definition of success. A great example of this was bungee jumping. It was a dream of mine to do it but I didn't have a particular place I wanted to do it in (even though I did envision it being on a tropical island). I thought that it would be somewhere abroad and I thought that it would cost a few hundred pounds (GBP) at the cheapest. I also thought that it was something that I'd only be able to do when I became rich.

I ended up doing it for a lot cheaper and far simpler than I thought possible. How? Well, I was making a point of sharing more of my bucket list goals to a couple of dear friends from university, when my friend Nikki just said matter of factly that not only can you do it in London, but you can do it for £50, due to wowcher (something that I could more than afford). She even sent me the coupon and I couldn't believe it. Finding out how cheap it was made the goal feel more real. Doing this however doesn't deal with the real issue, but it got a big obstacle out of the way.

Doing this also made me realise that not only do we use finance as an excuse to not achieve, but our definition of success is most probably cheaper than we thought it was. Achieving layers to your definition of success may not cost you any money at all.

EXERCISE #4 - BUCKET LIST MENU [WB PG 13]

Doing this also gave me a REAL reason to be financially responsible (not just because... 'it's the right thing to do'). From doing this I really understood how silly it was to use money as the main reason for not being successful

- 05 -
ACCEPTING YOUR ~~DEFINITION~~ VISION

Now that you have a clearer definition of success that is personal to you (which we will now call a vision). What is the next step? The next step is to accept it.

Ironically, acceptance is probably one of the biggest concepts that I found difficult to do on this journey. This is because...

1. I never truly understood what acceptance meant
2. I saw no difference between acceptance and giving up.

Acceptance doesn't mean giving up. From experience I've learnt that acceptance is actually the first step to changing something. Accepting the situation for what it is in the present moment, good, bad or indifferent. Even learning to accept the things that can't be changed allows you to be more focused on the things that you can change. During the times in my life when I felt down, I always held onto the idea that not only did I have the potential to be successful, but one day I will become successful. I would even use my visions of success as my escape route from my reality that I often found difficult to deal with.

I definitely wanted to fit in when growing up and I feel that all of us have either been through that stage or we still desire to fit in. What can be hard to accept is the idea that you may be different from what 'conventional wisdom' dictates that you should be. This is where the terrain can leave you in a sticky situation. One of the negative aspects of the power of people is that we can very easily get into a habit of defining ourselves in relation to other people we know. We may reassess ourselves as successful if someone we know becomes rich, or if someone gets married or if someone has a child. And to make it worse, we can also have people around us who define and compare us by other people we know (a great example of this is having one or both of your parents compare you to a brother or sister)

The biggest thing that I had to realise was that my definition of success was different to others around me. We may have wanted the same things, but I had to realise that some things were just more important to me than the others. Just this truth alone was difficult to accept. What is #23 on my list can be someone else's #1. I'm not driven by fame for example, if anything I see it as a hindrance to me living the type of life that I want. In comparison, another person can live solely to accomplish fame.

One of the reasons why was because of my concern that people would only want to be around me because of my fame, rather than who I really am (my real concern was that I wouldn't be able to tell the difference between the two, which we'll get deeper into later)

If you think someone being a millionaire is success, google 'unhappy millionaires' or 'unhappy successful people' and you will soon see that being a millionaire doesn't guarantee success. One of the biggest things I realised is that...

ACCEPTING YOUR DEFINITION OF SUCCESS MAY REQUIRE YOU TO ACCEPT THAT YOUR LIFE MAY HAVE TO CHANGE AND THERE ARE THINGS YOU ARE ATTACHED TO, THAT YOU MAY LOSE

Trying to accept your definition of success can produce many fears. Mine were:

- You aren't and will never be good enough to get it
- You will lose your sense of identity (Ego)
- **Your definition of success won't be accepted by the people whose approval you seek (therefore you will no longer be accepted)**

It's funny, because I have to admit to being scared of fear itself, but at the same time I can't recall any story of anyone successful where fear wasn't something that the person experienced and had to learn to deal with The next chapter will definitely touch on helping you accept your definition of success (as it did for me), but before I continue, I must say...

ACCEPT THE FACT THAT YOUR DEFINITION OF SUCCESS MAY CHANGE AS YOU GO ON YOUR JOURNEY, AND THAT'S OK

How you currently define success may change, and not only that, you may have to pursue that definition of success to then find out that your definition of success was truly something else. As a result, your bucket list and vision board may change over time, never mind your strategy(s) for achieving them. Feel free to change this as and when the time suits you. The most important thing about this is to get started and build momentum. Your definition of success may even change as you go through the rest of this book (as mine did whilst writing it and working through my reasons for not being successful... yet. The most important thing is that you are making time to accomplish success and happiness, when others are just waiting for it to happen.

EXERCISE #5 - THE VISION [WB PG 14]

GROUND ZERO - HABITUALS

By this point of the book you should have a good idea of what your vision looks like and you have something to work from. To facilitate the changes becoming long term instead of temporary, I came up with what I call Habituals for the end of this section and the other sections linked to my reasons for not being successful... yet. These are a mix of habits and rituals (and no I don't mean rituals in the witchcraft/wizardry sense). The idea was for them to be simple and non intrusive to one's current lifestyle. These will be at the end of each of the sections/reasons and whilst you are under no pressure to do these, I will say they massively helped me in my journey

1. Look over bucket list and vision board once a week minimum (5mins)
   a. Look at what you have already accomplished
   b. Look at what you haven't...yet
2. Evaluate bucket list and vision board - once a month
   a. Is this what I still want?
   b. Is this just as valuable as I saw it last month

REASON ONE:
I DON'T FEEL LIKE I'M GOOD ENOUGH

SIGNS & SYMPTOMS THAT YOU ARE SUFFERING FROM THIS INCLUDE, BUT ARE NOT LIMITED TO;

1. Taking things personally
2. Defining yourself by each and every outcome
3. Perfectionism
4. Violating and/or allowing others to violate your boundaries
5. Procrastination/Escapism

OBJECTIVE(S):

1. To identify one's reason(s) of not feeling good enough
2. To determine whether or not one is a perfectionist
3. To help develop/cultivate one's inner assertiveness
4. To help develop one's 'Tree of Good Enough'

My Truth

"For a very long time I've felt that I have to be perfect to be good enough. The only way that I could achieve what I wanted in life was to be perfect at all times. The second I made a mistake, it would mean the end of the world and I would lose everything that I deemed of any value.

And I believe this applied to everything, whether it was success in school, career, love or even socially. It would be bad enough if I saw this that as a principle that applied to everyone, but I feel that this principle only applies to me. My upbringing, but more importantly how I chose to respond to this upbringing, has been a massive influence in this way of thinking

As a result, I would often be bitter and resentful at others who achieved what I wanted, especially those that I perceived were further away from this idea of perfection than me.

Throughout my childhood, I was always labelled as a bright and gifted kid that was meant for great things. I could grasp the concept of things pretty quickly and could often figure things out without much instruction from others. I was even told at the age of 7 that I had a photographic memory by one of my teachers. My response to this was to attach my sense of self (and thus self confidence) to this idea. I developed a need to feel like the smartest person in the room and whenever I was in the presence of anyone who I felt was more gifted and/or smarter than me, I would be intimidated and distance myself from them and/or the situation.

I felt like I could achieve anything I ever wanted AND I didn't have to try as hard as other people. I felt a sense of superiority and also a state of calm, whereby I believed that all I ever needed to achieve the things I wanted in the world was to turn on the desire to do so (like a light switch) and not only will it happen, it will happen easily. I also developed very high standards, but it came with a caveat. Whenever I achieved my standards, I would immediately downplay my achievement and even question whether the standard was truly high at all (especially because I achieved it). Additionally, my self defence mechanism I would use when I felt like I wouldn't be able to meet my high standard, was pulling back my best effort so that I would have the ready made excuse that 'I didn't really try". What would break my heart would be when I didn't meet my standards in a situation where I actually tried my hardest.

Coming to think of it, I feel that I have lived my life by protecting this self image of myself. Whenever I came across something, whether it was a computer game, a life skill or project that became too difficult, I would abandon it (and would rationalise by saying I didn't want to do it anymore)

A thought process that I've had for some time (and one that took me many years to realise) was the belief that If I truly was good enough "I would have been successful by now". The idea that I would try to accomplish something to then discover that I missed my window of opportunity feels beyond daunting to me. Even more daunting is the idea that I could discover that I never was good enough and I've lived the majority of my life believing a lie. I was more fearful with how I would deal with this reality than the reality itself.

My favourite way of dealing with this was procrastination and avoidance. When I was younger, it would be with computer games and surfing online. Now that I'm older, it's anything that makes me feel comfortable and at ease, like watching tv, films or anything that will distract me."

06

PRELUDE 1: DEALING WITH PERFECTIONISM

NB: If you don't think you are a perfectionist, read this section anyway just in case you are. And if you truly aren't, well good for you, you have less work than the rest of us :)

> *"Perfectionism becomes a badge of honour with you playing the part of the suffering hero"*
>
> David D Burns

Perfectionism is a disease. That's my thoughts on it in one sentence. I either wanted to be perfect or nothing. I never saw value in being mediocre, or even excellent. I had ridiculously high standards when I was younger. The younger version of myself would argue that it came from being told by others that I was destined for great things, but having high standards is a beautiful thing.

What took me decades to understand was that what's of more value is not only how I deal with my high standards, but how I deal with NOT meeting my high standards.

The first heartbreak I can remember was during primary school in year 6 (for those of you who aren't familiar with the british school system, this is the year just before you go to secondary school (ages 10-11yrs). Mr Garnham was my teacher and we would have a star system. It was primarily based on the weekly spelling test of 10 words each week and whoever got the best score on the test would receive a star. Whoever got the most stars by the end of the year would win. Every kid in the class' name was written on a chart. Every single week I would be fixated on getting the best spelling score and would often get all 10 words spelt correctly. I was so far away and ahead of all my classmates. It filled me with great pride. Then on one occasion I got a word wrong...ONE WRONG WORD...

I can't even remember what the word was, but I do remember crying like a baby during the following lunch time. It was like my whole entire sense of self esteem shattered into a million pieces. To make matters worse there was a girl called Leanne who was catching up to me on the star chart. It was neck and neck between us and I don't remember getting another spelling test wrong after that. I was convinced that I was going to win. And then something happened that to this day irritates me. Leanne got an extra star for her homework... something that no one ever got. I was absolutely stunned, angry and bitter. Leanne was a nice girl to be fair and my issue was never with her. It was with my teacher Mr Garnham (ironically my favourite teacher). I felt like I played the game almost perfectly and yet I got punished for making one mistake. On top of this I felt like I lost in a game that I had no chance in winning. This was probably the first experience which I concluded that I HAD to be perfect to deserve what I truly want.

Perfectionism is an interesting concept because there are people who would debate on whether it is beneficial or destructive. Just as much as there is a group of people who are convinced that perfectionism has held them back from being successful, I'm pretty sure there is another group who would say their desire to be perfect is what made them as successful as they became (e.g. athletes)

I reacted to how I was raised by holding the belief that if you are going to try something, you have to be perfect, and if you can't envision yourself being perfect then don't bother trying. As a silent middle finger to perfectionism, this part of the book may be the most imperfect part...

EXERCISE #6 THE PERFECTIONIST'S QUESTIONNAIRE (FOR PERFECTIONISTS' ONLY) [WB PG 18]

This questionnaire is more of a reflection on my relationship with perfectionism. And as you can imagine when I asked myself these questions, I realised how ineffective perfectionism was in my pursuit of success. The biggest reason why is because it stopped me from doing something that has a direct correlation with success...TRYING.

"The difference between the Student and the Master is that the Master has failed more times than the Student has ever tried"

Come to find out that quote came from Master Yoda and Star Wars (I don't even like Star Wars). Even though it came from a film, it brings with it a great point. This is what made me discover the first principle that I outlined in this book. In case you have forgotten...

TO WIN IS TO TRY

Any school of thought or belief system that stops you from even trying is not only dangerous, but it robs you of the opportunity to grow and progress. So if perfectionism is futile, what should one pursue instead? The answer is Good Enough, that's it. And just in case you read it wrong, one should pursue being good enough rather than perfection. The four pillars of good enough are Self Esteem, Self Confidence, Confidence and Insecurities, all of which very much overlap with each other. Good enough will be discussed a little later, but firstly one needs to cover...

07

Internal Personal Boundaries (I.P.B)

"Your personal boundaries protect the inner core of your identity and your right to choices"

Gerard Manley Hopkins

Before this journey I thought I was amazing with boundaries. I had always been respectful of boundaries (even if I didn't agree with it). I did feel though that I could always be the exception to a boundary and would love trying to charm my way into being an exception (rather than maliciously violating a boundary). On the other hand though, from this journey I didn't realise how important **personal** boundaries are (I didn't even know there was a difference between the two). The textbook definition of a boundary is 'a line which marks the limits of an area; a dividing line'. This definition is only a fraction of the story. By personal boundaries I mean the following:

1. A personal rule that yourself and/or others need to abide by
2. A personal right that you want to protect
3. Established consequence(s) to violation of personal rule
4. Reasonable exception(s) to the rule (if necessary).
5. Communication of that personal rule
6. You enforce the consequence(s) to ANY and EVERY violation

Put bluntly, I soon realised that I am a shambles when it comes to personal boundaries. By this definition of the term, I can truly admit to having difficulty with this. This was important to understand because If I have issues with abiding by my own personal boundaries for myself, it doesn't bode well for other people abiding by my personal boundaries. Another truth to be told is that one's adeptness with boundaries has a massive impact on feeling good enough.

Put simply, I'd argue there are two types of personal boundaries, across 5 different categories:

Types of Personal Boundary
1. Internal - Boundaries that YOU set for YOURSELF to abide by (IPB)
2. External - Boundaries that YOU set for OTHERS to abide by (EPB)

Boundary Categories
1. Physical
   a. Health
   b. Time
   c. Space
   d. Objects/Possessions
2. Mental - Thoughts
3. Emotional - Feelings
4. Spiritual - Values

External personal boundaries are the most commonly known type of boundary and will be covered in Reason 3. However, it's of more value to establish and become good at enforcing one's internal personal boundaries. If you struggle to abide by your own boundaries, the challenge of having other people abide by your boundaries is going to be even greater.

With that being said, finding this out alone didn't help so much. I had always put others before myself (which I feel is an admirable quality), however doing so, at your own expense, is simply unhealthy. I realised how much doing so affected my sense of self worth and value. Learning to set boundaries felt necessary but overwhelming. I had to truly understand the nature of boundaries. I previously thought that boundaries were to cater to what you desired, but I actually discovered ...

THE PURPOSE OF BOUNDARIES ARE TO PROTECT YOUR <u>RIGHTS</u>, NOT JUST YOUR NEEDS, WANTS OR DESIRES

This would explain why I had difficulty setting them (especially if I have been putting the needs, wants or desires of others above my own) So the next step is to establish my rights, but how?...

I.P.B. DETOUR: KNOW YOUR RIGHTS

"You can't fight for your rights if you don't know what they are"
John Roberts

Whenever the topic of rights comes up, people normally only think about human and legal rights. That's because it's the most common context in which they are discussed. In this book however, I'm talking about personal rights. Ironically enough, before I even got into personal rights I realised that a lot of us don't even know all of our human and legal rights. The violation of human rights you mostly hear on the news in relation to a crime a country makes, rather than that of a crime that humans make. To violate someone's human rights is one of the worst crimes any human can commit in my opinion, and yet many of us only view our human rights in regards to simply survival, rather than overall wellbeing.

Previously, I had seen my rights as primitive (e.g. access to clean drinking water, access to minimum wage employment, etc). Here is a non exhaustive list of what I consider to be one's personal rights (provided that no one is harmed, no laws are being broken and/or no one else's rights are being violated)

1. To be safe (physically, mentally, emotionally and spiritually).

2. To be respected

3. To be treated fairly.

4. To have needs & wants.

5. To listen to my intuition.

6. To ask for what I feel I need and/or want.

7. To try.

8. To make a decision.

9. To say 'yes'

10. To say 'no'

11. To be unsure

12. To change a decision.

13. To make a mistake.

14. To express myself (thoughts, feelings & values)

15. To forgive myself.

16. To forgive others.

17. To express emotion

18. To have a code of honour, or a set of values

19. To be happy & enjoy life, as I see fit.

20. To improve and/or try to improve

21. To be honest

22. To agree or disagree with someone else

23. To become the best version of myself, as I see fit"

This list inspired the next exercise that I did.

EXERCISE #7 - PERSONAL RIGHTS QUESTIONNAIRE [WB PG 20]

Doing this exercise was truly enlightening. I no longer felt guilty about having needs, wants and desires, and felt stronger about protecting what I had soon realised were my rights. That being said, I felt that I had to go through a process of making these rights simpler to remember and more personal to me. From this I realised that not only did I not have, but I need a personal bill of rights. A personal bill of rights is simply a list of rights that you intend to honour and will ensure that others respect (or face appropriate consequences). The more personal they are, the better. This is simply because the more connected you are to them, the harder you will fight for them. I implore you to do the same.

EXERCISE #8 - PERSONAL BILL OF RIGHTS [WB PG 22]

Rewording these rights in a way that resonated with me had me feeling not only embarrassed but grateful for getting real insight into how much of a factor this has been in my life. The stage next from establishing personal rights is to establish Internal Personal Boundaries (IPB) so that I can properly protect my personal rights. Upon reflection, I realised my only real I.P.Bs before this journey were:

1. Don't violate the boundaries of others
2. Put the boundaries of others before your own

I actually grew up thinking that boundaries were something that was imposed on you, rather than realising that boundaries are things you also have the power to set for yourself. Here is a checklist I put together for determining whether or not you have an I.P.B.

- ☐ The Boundary (in a sentence)
- ☐ One or more clear right the boundary is designed to protect
- ☐ You have communicated it to yourself (in writing or via self talk)
- ☐ A consequence to violation of that boundary
- ☐ Pre-Established exception(s) to the boundary
- ☐ History of communicating and enforcing those boundaries

Example: Gabriel and his intermittent fasting eating habits

Gabriel wants to lose weight and is going to be doing intermittent fasting (a concept where those involved would eat in a short window during the day and fast for the rest of the day). Following the checklist, here is Michael's boundary:

1. No food or drink after 6pm each day
2. Gabriel's right to be healthy (and to be healthier than those around him)
3. If Gabriel violates the rule, he would have to do 30 push ups (the most he can do in one sitting is 20)
4. Drinking water is the only exception to the boundary
5. Gabriel wrote it down in his journal
6. On one occasion, Gabriel drank a fizzy drink later on in the evening and subsequently did 30 push ups over 30mins in 2 sittings (which he hated)

I learned that the reason you need to be clear on which right the boundary is protecting is because if you don't know what you are protecting, it is worthless. In addition, the boundary should be an extension of the right you seek to protect. You must communicate this to yourself, as this is a great way of committing to it, (in similar fashion to writing your desired goals on paper.) A consequence for violating the boundary is truly what makes this work (especially for me). If you don't have established consequences for your boundaries, you don't have as much incentive to honour them, which will affect your sense of good enough (which will be discussed later). Another element that is necessary is having a consequence in place if you don't actually go through with the violation of the boundary. My way of doing this was having the fine(s) I place double whenever I didn't log down and/or pay the first fine. This was inspired by governments, who do this all the time to incentivise people to pay fines promptly (e.g. driving tickets, public transport fines, etc). This is also designed to condition you into understanding that things can get worse if you don't take accountability for your violations.

EXERCISE #9 - I.P.B CHART [WB PG 23]

The final element is to have and maintain records of your IPBs, any time you have violated it and also any time that you have failed to enforce the consequence for violating your boundary promptly enough. This is VITAL!!! Having your own records of this is what helped me get a lot better at feeling good enough. I did this in the form of what I call an I.P.B Violation Record. This is a record of all the times that you violated your own I.P.B and the consequences attached to it. This was designed to help me hold myself accountable. The consequences for violating your boundary can be anything but it has to be something that will motivate you to honour your boundary.

Guidance: There are many examples of consequences you can impose on yourself. In case you are having issues with which ones to do, I'll tell you what I did. I created a system where there were a range of financial penalties for each boundary violation (as losing money is a form of motivation I resonate with to honour my boundary(s). That penalty was to take the form of a donation to a charity I absolutely despised. I researched them to find that they have a minimum donation which was larger than my financial penalties. I then created a system where I recorded each violation, but I didn't have to pay a donation to the charity until all my penalties totalled the minimum donation amount. This worked great because there were many instances where I violated my boundaries and even though I felt punished, I also felt like I got a chance to correct my behaviour before I would really suffer.

EXERCISE #10 - I.P.B VIOLATION RECORD [WB PG 25]

PS: Find charity(s) that allow you to donate anonymously if you are going to follow my system.

This is a great primer for the rest of my journey and to be honest, If there was any one thing I would want to share from my journey that I hope you learn from, it would be this. And from this point I truly established a value that I had discovered some time before.

VALUE #2: TREAT <u>YOURSELF</u> THE WAY YOU WANT TO BE TREATED

Previously, I believed and was raised to believe in treating others the way you want to be treated (like countless others), but I soon realised that this didn't result in the outcomes I wanted. Nobody was really treating me as well as I liked to treat others. From work, to my personal life (yes that includes dating). As the saying goes; 'if you don't' believe in yourself, who will?'. I believe the same applies to loving and caring for yourself. Outside of possibly your parents/guardians (before you become an adult), nobody can and should care for and love you more than you do. It took me a while, but I eventually understood that the people who were treated the best by others were those who would treat themselves better than others would.

One of the best ways to treat yourself well is to establish boundaries for you to abide by that are designed to protect your personal rights. If you can't do that, what chance do you have with establishing boundaries for others to abide by?

- 08 -
GAINING PERSPECTIVE: WHAT IS GOOD ENOUGH?

"Good enough is the new perfect"

Becky Beaupre Gillespie

The most ironic thing about it all is that my goal was to be good enough this entire time. I'd even argue that we all as humans desire to be good enough, rather than perfect. The only question I thought was necessary to answer was; 'good enough for what?'

BEING GOOD ENOUGH IS RELATIVE TO WHAT YOUR DEFINITION OF SUCCESS IS

I however feel that this is half true. The reason I say that is because what if you don't know what your definition of success is? The above statement would imply that you would have to know what your definition of success is before you can become good enough. Uncertainty is a big part of reality and I wanted to be good enough to deal with any and every possible situation. I truly believe it is unhealthy to base your self esteem on outcomes, but this came from realising how much I was suffering from doing just that. It was also at this point that I realised that I would have to learn to base my self esteem on something healthier than perfection.

Then I had to ask myself the questions. "What is actually good enough? Just asking myself this question was a challenge. After much soul searching I realised.

GOOD ENOUGH IS A STATE OF MIND WHERE YOU KNOW YOU ARE WORTHY OF UNCONDITIONAL SELF AND/OR EXTERNAL LOVE REGARDLESS OF WHO YOU WERE, ARE OR WILL BECOME

Admit it, you were expecting a more linear definition of good enough, did-n't you? Why on earth have I come up with this definition? The reason why is because being good enough is simply not linear. Of course there are lin-ear aspects of good enough, for example, you would need to study at university for a number of years before you could become qualified as a doctor (regardless of how much you believe in yourself). That being said, good enough starts before that moment. For you to go through the process of being a doctor (which can take many hard years to achieve), you would need a very strong resolve before going through it and an even stronger re-solve during the process.

With that being said, I had to first work through this concept in the linear sense to truly understand the abstract part of this concept. Thinking about this in the linear sense also makes it easy to do something about becoming good enough. That of course will bring the question...

"How close to or far away am I from being good enough?"

But I think when we think about good enough, we ask ourselves the follow-ing (whether we realise it or not)...

1. Am I actually good enough to accomplish this now?
2. If I'm not yet, how close to or far away am I from being good enough?
3. What is the process I would have to go through to be good enough?
4. Do I feel like I am good enough to go through the process?
5. Do I feel the process is worth my time and effort?

I realised that what I struggled with the most was the fourth question. My response whenever I would answer no to the fourth question was to not bother trying. Questions 1 and 3 can be found through simple research. Question 2 is a challenging question that is better answered by people around you rather than only yourself (as it can be an emotionally challenging, but rewarding task). Question 5 is addressed in detail in Reason 4 of the book.

Let's start with questions 1 and 2. Even though I am blessed to have many people in my life who are prepared to help me, asking for help is something that I just didn't feel comfortable doing (more on that in Reason 3). So how could I go about finding the answers to question 1 & 2 without getting help from others?

IDENTIFY PEOPLE WHO YOU CONSIDER TO BE 'GOOD ENOUGH'

Going through this process is what made me realise the importance of knowing what my definition of success is (or so I thought). If I didn't know what it was, or had a starting point to further explore it, there was no way I could define whether I was good enough or not. I was reluctant at first to identify people I considered to be good enough. This was because:

1. I'm pretty sure there are people I personally know who would be in this list (which would bruise my ego and possibly create resentment)
2. I might feel like these people were a level beyond my capability
3. I might actually feel bad, because the people may not be as good as me (which would mean that I've wasted all this time living in fear and doubting myself)

The reason why identifying people is important is because it opens your mind to actual reality; not what you perceive reality to be. You may feel like burying your head in the sand on this one, but that's a good thing, as it's a chance for you to develop your courage (this entire process for me was scary)

Before continuing, it is important to establish some categories to your life. There are many different categories but for the sake of simplicity I will name 5 that truly helped me to focus, which came courtesy of Jeff Olson, in his book the Slight Edge (another book I truly recommend reading). These categories are:

- Health
- Wealth
- Relationships
- Happiness
- Personal Growth/Development

You get to decide which of these categories are most important to you. You also get to change your mind over time as your priorities can change at the speed of life. Dedicating time to these categories in your life will lead to you feeling a more fulfilling life. It is thus important to recognise that your definition of good enough can also apply definitely to each of these categories. You may even realise that you have different people who are good enough to you in those different categories.

EXERCISE #11 - GOOD ENOUGH LIST [WB PG 27]

YOU DON'T EVER HAVE TO BE PERFECT TO BE GOOD ENOUGH

I would previously associate 'good enough' with 'mediocre', 'average' and 'just about'. I never wanted to be mediocre in anything and with pursuing perfection it presented me with the opportunity to show the world how special I felt like I was. Now I realise the complete opposite

From a linear definition, Good enough is the **minimum** needed to meet a goal or standard, however I am also referring to 'Good Enough' as a philosophy. The previous philosophy I pursued was that of perfection. So the question is; why should anyone abandon the pursuit of Perfection for the pursuit of Good Enough?

GOOD ENOUGH VS PERFECT

From my experience the most significant benefit to pursuing good enough rather than perfection is you will save time and energy. Time and energy are probably the most useful gifts you'll ever receive

Another benefit to pursuing good enough over perfect is the mere fact that you would be nurturing one of humanity's greatest desires; to grow.

EXAMPLE: MICHAEL AND MICHELLE: WHO DO YOU THINK DOES BETTER?

Michael and Michelle are both university students and are looking at past exam papers to help with their final exams, which is two months away. The final exams and all previous exams contained 5 questions each. There are four exam papers in total from previous years and their lecturer has told them to practice all four papers because their final exam will contain a mix of questions from each (of which no priority paper out of the four has been established).

Michael focuses on previous exam paper 1 and resolves to move onto previous exam paper 2, 3 and 4 only when he gets 100% on exam paper 1. Michael hits a wall at 85% and ends up taking time off procrastinating, then getting back to it. What's more important to him is being perfect in each exam paper before moving on, regardless of what it takes. He gets to 100% in exam paper 1 and completely shifts focus to exam paper 2, eventually gets to 100% with barely any time to get to 100% on exam paper 3. By the final exam, Michael has spent the majority of his time on Exam paper 1 & 2, but nowhere near as much time as 3 & 4 (the latter he didn't have the time to work on at all).

Michelle on the other hand decides to focus on exam paper 1 until she gets 70% and swiftly moves on to 2,3, and 4. Michelle hits a wall at 60% and decides to spend time on exam paper 2 as a form of active rest before going back to exam paper 1. Michelle gets to a point where she's working on all four exam papers simultaneously until the final exam

What's more important to her is being good enough in all four exam papers.

So who are you going for? Michael or Michelle?

Most of you would say Michelle, and you would be right. However some of you might feel

<u>"Michael focused on achieving 100% in every paper,</u>
<u>what are you talking about?"</u>

That is of course possible and even if he didn't know, Michael could strike it lucky and most of the questions could end up being from paper 1 and 2. That being said, how likely is that to be the case in this example?

By chasing perfection, Michael has put himself in a situation where he's anxious, as he needs the final exam to have the majority of the questions from exam paper 1 & 2, whereas Michelle is comfortable either way. Michael studied in a style where he needs the circumstances to be 'perfect' (the majority of the questions coming from papers 1 & 2) to achieve success. Michelle on the other hand studied in a way where the circumstances aren't going to drastically affect her chances of succeeding.

And if there was one sole point of this book that I would want you to walk away from is understanding the value in the mindset that you will succeed, regardless of your circumstances.

How Do You Know When You Are Good Enough?: The Tests & Criteria of Good Enough

For me, the short answer to this question is of the following criteria...

1. **Vision:** Your readiness to imagine
2. **Drive:** Your readiness to TRY
3. **Accountability:** How you react when things DON'T go your way
4. **Resilience & Adaptability:** Your readiness to KEEP TRYING UNTIL YOU SUCCEED (even if it means changing paths)
5. **Interdependence:** Your readiness to get HELP from & work with others
6. **Competition:** How you react to COMPETITION & your readiness to COMPETE
7. **Gratitude:** How you react when things DO go your way

Below are a series of guide questions for each criteria. You can make a point to directly answer each question, however they are more designed to help you gauge whether or not you possess each criteria.

Vision: Your readiness to imagine
Guide Questions

- *Can you imagine the ideal outcome or life for yourself?*
- *Do you experience any self doubt when imagining this ideal outcome or life?*
- *Can you still imagine the ideal outcome or life for yourself, in spite of any self doubt?*

<u>Drive:</u> Your readiness to TRY
Guide Questions

- *Do you get anxious at the idea of trying something?*
- *Do you anticipate failure?*
- *Do you anticipate success?*
- *Are you still prepared to try, in spite of any anxiety or negative emotion?*

Accountability: How you react when things DON'T go your way
Guide Questions

- *Do you get angry or sulk?*
- *Do you take it personally and consider yourself a failure or bad human being?*
- *Do you feel bitterness or resentment towards others that you perceive have experienced things going their way when you haven't?*
- *Do you give up?*
- *Do you blame others before you blame yourself?*
- *Do you see the opportunity(s) for growth that this moment presents?*
- *Do you feel gratitude for the experience?*

Resilience & Adaptability: Your readiness to TRY AGAIN & TRY DIFFERENT (if necessary)
Guide Questions

- *Do you feel crippled by self doubt by the thought of trying again because of the failure from your first/previous attempt?*
- *Are you scared that achieving your desired outcome will take too many attempts?*
- *Are you scared to try a different way of achieving the same result?*
- *Are you scared to consider that your path may have to change?*
- *Are you able to pivot from your chosen path if it means getting to your definition of success?*

Interdependence: Your readiness to get help
<u>Guide Questions</u>

- *Are you reluctant to get help?*
- *Do you feel like you can figure it out on your own?*
- *Do you feel like you have to do something on your own for the achievement to be of any value?*
- *Do you feel getting help forever condemns you to be lesser than?*
- *Do you feel like you are beyond help?*

Competition: How you react to COMPETITION and your readiness to COMPETE
<u>Guide Questions</u>

- *Do you feel excited or threatened by competition?*
- *When you sense there is competition for what you want, do you lose belief in yourself and withdraw?*
- *Does competition trigger your desire to improve?*
- *Does the outcome have to be guaranteed for you to feel comfortable competing?*
- *Do you see competing as only worth it when you win? Or do you see it as a win-win regardless of the result?*
- *Does your enjoyment of competing depend solely on whether you win or lose?*
- *Can you compete again straight after 'losing'?*

Gratitude: How you react when things DO go your way
<u>Guide Questions</u>

- *Do you get arrogant or entitled when things go your way and always expect for this to continue?*
- *Do you get complacent and feel like you don't have to put in as much effort for the same outcome?*

- *Do you act like it was a fluke when things go your way?*
- *Do you think your goals aren't challenging enough whenever you achieve them?*
- *Do you celebrate your milestones?*
- *Do you pat yourself on the back and gracefully move to the next milestone?*
- *Or do you just continue onto the next thing like nothing happened?*
- *Do you express gratitude to those that helped in things going your way?*
- *Do you feel gratitude for circumstances that facilitated things going your way?*

The answer to addressing these criteria is working on what I've mentioned earlier… Self Esteem, Self Confidence, Confidence & Insecurities. For many people, self esteem, self confidence and confidence are one in the same, but that simply isn't true and there is a nuance. So what is the difference?

SELF ESTEEM = YOUR SENSE OF SELF WORTH/VALUE
SELF CONFIDENCE = YOUR PERSONAL QUALITY(S)
CONFIDENCE = YOUR SKILLS

Having realised the difference between the three, I immediately understood how easy it is to have one without the other. Without self esteem, I could have the qualities & skills I needed but I'd never feel like I deserve what I have or want. Without self confidence, I can feel hollow in the sense that I feel I deserve what I have but I feel like something is missing. Without confidence I can easily feel like a fraud or charlatan, AKA Imposter Syndrome (which can also be caused by low self esteem)

SIDEBAR - Many people see qualifications and skills as synonymous. Qualifications imply you have the skills but it's simply not always true,

ask employers how they feel about hiring recent university gradu-
ates...)

How do I know I'm adequate in each one? The answer is...

When you feel positive or not particularly bothered whenever any of the tests happen.

1. Your readiness to TRY and TRY AGAIN

You have no problem trying and trying again.

2. How you react when things DO go your way

You credit yourself, celebrate the moment, look for any learning lessons &
move on to the next step

3. How you react when things DON'T go your way

You hold yourself accountable, are able to be held accountable by others
without feeling violated/offended & look for opportunity(s) to grow,
whilst being receptive to feedback from others.

4. Your readiness to get HELP

You quickly identify when help would add value (not just when it is
needed) and you actively seek it.

5. How you react to COMPETITION & your readiness to COMPETE

You get excited by and identify growth opportunities from your competition and their qualities that help you grow.

Here is a question I want to throw at you... If you were told by someone
that you are going to achieve your definition of success within a time frame

that you were comfortable with, regardless of the obstacles in your way, how would you deal with the tests of good enough? Life experience has taught me that we often react badly to things that happen when we feel we can't or don't want to deal with the anticipated consequences. In addition, life has taught me that the majority of things we worry about actually don't come to pass.

What helped me was choosing to believe the following...

EVERYTHING THAT HAPPENS TO YOU IS DESIGNED TO HELP YOU ACHIEVE YOUR DEFINITION OF SUCCESS, BUT IT'S FOR YOU TO FIGURE OUT HOW

For those of you who are religious, you may have noticed how common it is for some people to have a somewhat transactional relationship with their religious deity. Growing up in a Christian environment, it would often feel like people were praying to God for things like they were ordering from a menu. I'd much rather pray to God by expressing gratitude for what he has already given and continues to give to me. How can you ask for new things to receive if you don't express gratitude for the things you have already received? That being said, it's also important to ask for what you want. The reason why is that God/Allah/The Universe/Insert other religious deity that apply to you here (whichever you believe, to me though they are one in the same) can create pathways for you to walk through. The problem though is we often aren't clear on what we want and yet we get frustrated when we don't receive clear pathways.

Now we understand the criteria for good enough, what would these tests of good enough look like in real life?

1. **Try**
    o   You are faced in a situation where there is something you need to try to achieve an outcome that is important to you.

2. **Try Again**
   - o You are faced in a situation where you tried and failed to achieve an outcome that was important to you.
3. **Things going your way**
   - o You accomplished the outcome you wanted, exactly how you wanted it (e.g. achieving something first time trying)
4. **Things not going your way**
   - o In an attempt to achieve an outcome, you feel like nothing you are doing is getting you closer to achieving it
5. **Help**
   - o You are struggling to achieve an outcome to the point where you feel you can't do it on your own
     - i. Organising a birthday party
6. **Competition**
   - o You are trying to achieve the same outcome that many others want to achieve, where only a few of you can achieve it (at the expense of others)
     - i. E.g. Job Interview

The rest of this section of the book is designed to help fly through the tests of good enough.

09

R.O.G.E - ROOTS OF GOOD ENOUGH (SELF ESTEEM)

"I got 19 years of: 'No', 'Not good enough', You don't get the part'. You don't
need permission of a higher level to make you feel that you can do what you
want to do"

Kevin Hart

Just like the tree in life would be defined and start with the roots, the tree of good enough is the same. In short, the value I chose to create and live by is...

VALUE #3: I'M ALREADY GOOD ENOUGH (TO START AT THE VERY LEAST)

You are already good enough to start your journey. Right here & right now. And if there were any scenarios where you actually weren't good enough to arrive at a destination/milestone, then you are good enough to learn to be. With this I had to unlearn previous unhelpful and untrue beliefs, but how did these untrue beliefs take shape?

In a similar way that I'm convinced that we are born to have hate for no-one, not feeling good enough is a direct consequence of beliefs we have picked up externally. Whether that be our environment or taking on the attitudes of our family and/or friends (similar to how a child can develop racist attitudes by being around racist/racially insensitive parents). You may have noticed at this point that my definition of Good Enough sounds pretty similar to self belief/confidence, and you would be right.

I had to learn that anyone can learn anything, absolutely anything. There is simply too much evidence in human history to counter my previous belief (just the idea of a blind person being able to learn and play piano at an elite level should be all the proof you need; cough, Stevie Wonder, cough)

I started on this journey by asking myself

1. How am I already good enough?
2. If not, What do I need to learn to be Good Enough?

And from here I developed a concept called R.O.G.E. (Roots of Good Enough).

I began to see good enough as a tree with many leaves, branches and roots. With it I can strengthen my Tree of Good Enough by unearthing old roots and cultivating new roots. This process is about identifying what about you right now (without any additional work) qualifies you to be good enough. Similar to Reason 0 (where you may find out that you are already further ahead than you thought you were) you might actually be good enough or closer to it than you thought, when you may have previously felt that you were nowhere near good enough. Doing this made my mind shift and my perspective changed to a more positive outlook.

EXERCISE #12 - R.O.G.E. CHART [WB PG 29]

I hope you now feel as good as I did when I did this exercise. However, what if I was the exception that proves the rule? How else could I measure my level of good enough? If you have completed the first section you would be aware of the concept and value of having a bucket list. As valuable as it is, it is an incomplete exercise, and doesn't tell the whole picture in one's story.

This is the time when I thought about all the things that I have achieved, rather than just focusing on the things that I haven't achieved…yet.

EXERCISE #13 - 'ALREADY DONE' BUCKET LIST [WB PG 30]

How do you feel? When I looked back at my list I was actually taken aback. I've actually accomplished more things (that truly mattered to me) than I gave myself credit for. There were times when I would mention some of my accomplishments to people close to me in general conversation and I would play it off as a small thing, but their eyes would light up at some of my accomplishments.

The reason I did this was because my definition of success was based on what I hadn't accomplished, rather than an accurate picture of what I hadn't but what I had also accomplished. Doing this allowed me to truly assess my life so far, and it wasn't as bad as I previously thought. For those of you that have achieved some of the things that you've always wanted to; well done and pat yourself on the back, as you've taken an important step in your journey. For those of you that haven't, I hope the exercise sharpens your mind to work towards what truly matters to you.

Now we've dealt with cultivating the roots, let's have a look at the next state...the branches.

10

B.O.G.E - BRANCHES OF GOOD ENOUGH (SELF CONFIDENCE)

"We cannot become what we want by remaining who we are"

Max De Pree

Self esteem is paramount to any level of success, but it would be naive to believe that is all you need. Everything worth having requires a range of skills and qualities (many of which need to be cultivated over time) to achieve. This part of the book is about working on one's self confidence. Remember the difference established between the two earlier in the book? Just like the branches and roots of a tree, self esteem and self confidence work very much hand in hand. However similar they may be, they are different. This is where you'll better understand (just like I had to) how much so. Truly understanding the difference between the two will help strengthen both. Often people have solely focused on growing their self confidence and it has resulted in masking their low self esteem, and vice versa.

The added value of working on your branches of good enough, is that it can either confirm your definition of success, or it may even make you change course and tweak it. My personal belief is that the qualities that you identify as increasing your chances of achieving this need to be qualities that you either already have or qualities that you are excited by the idea of developing. If you desire to have children but have no patience, whilst having no desire to develop this quality, then you should question whether or not having children is truly part of your definition of success (side bar: if you appreciate the importance of patience but don't feel you have it, a work around would be having patience as a natural quality that you would seek in your life partner to help provide balance to the upbringing of any children you were to raise).

In this example, you can see how developing a greater understanding of these branches can also help you with your strategy when it comes to achieving your definition of success. So what value did I adopt to help with this...

VALUE #4: ACTION BEFORE SELF CONFIDENCE

You may have noticed a subtle difference between the value I used to help with my self esteem and the one I used for self confidence. Self esteem is about realising that you are worthy and of value right now (as all humans are) and regularly reminding yourself of that in a world that can profit from helping you forget. With self confidence however, it's more about learning and developing skills & gaining experience that are required to deliver your definition of success. Please note what I said about skills, as I want to make a clear distinction between self confidence and confidence.

If you were to once again imagine a tree, Self Esteem is the roots, Self Confidence is the branches and Confidence is the leaves. Confidence in this context are just leaves, which are nice to have, but if they have no connection to the branches and the roots they will wither and die. By this same token, you can acquire many skills in life, but if they have no connection to your definition of success or have no importance to you, it's pretty useless. A great example is someone who sees getting married and having well educated, high achieving children as their definition of success, who is great at online gaming during their spare time but is average at their job and horrible at dating.

So how do I work on self confidence? The short answer is to fall in love with lifelong learning and growth, regularly identifying qualities that you feel will increase your chances of achieving your definition of success, whilst enjoying the process of cultivating those same qualities that may not have.

The first step is to identify the qualities that can increase your chances of achieving your definition of success. So how do I identify these qualities? At this point of my journey I remembered something that my first music mentor told me all the way back in 2003, which is the same thing I got £20k+ in student loan debt to learn.

GOOGLE IS YOUR FRIEND

If there is one thing that we as a society have to be more grateful for in this era, it has to be how much easier it is to find information and high quality information. Once upon a time (for those of you old enough to remember) we had to look for information via the library and encyclopaedias. Encyclopaedias in particular were not only very expensive but you would have to invest in them on a regular basis, as information was always being updated, whilst later on there used to be CD versions of encyclopaedias (who remembers Encarta?).

The trade off to there being more available information is that we as a society had to improve our ability to screen and separate good information from the bad (the one good thing going to university done for me). Literally anyone can put any information online now, whereas in previous generations, professionals with a high level of credentials were the only authors accepted anywhere near an encyclopaedia. Now you can run a simple google search on the qualities and skills you need. But here is my process when it comes to finding information:

1. Run a search (e.g. qualities needed to be a music producer)
2. Read 3-4 articles minimum
3. Identify the consensus (that the articles have in common)
4. If possible, run information by someone you know who would know (e.g. a friend of yours who happens to be a music producer)

The last two steps are vital because they help separate good information from the bad. Search engines run by algorithms that rank information and websites, relative to search queries, by its relevance and popularity. It would often do this by having the best quality sources at the top of a search (or at the very least the first page of the search results) This system however isn't perfect due to one's ability to influence themselves and their information being at the top of relevant search results (e.g. via Search Engine Optimisation). In addition, it's just good practice to read across many sources to identify true information and knowledge (another skill that university taught me: still not sure if it was worth the price though, but that's another conversation for another book). Finally reading the same thing from multiple sources will also boost your confidence in the information.

EXERCISE #14 - BRANCH FINDER [WB PG 32]

Just being aware of my branches made me feel liberated and a lot more focused. I recognised what I already had and doing the research made me feel good, as it confirmed my initial instincts. There were also qualities that I can accept I'm not good at currently. At the same time I'm excited by the idea of learning to cultivate them. If there is anything that I would want you to take from this part of the book is that you don't have to have the qualities already, but you should like and look forward to the idea of learning to develop those qualities.

11

L.O.G.E: LEAVES OF GOOD ENOUGH

"Repetition is the mother of skill"

Tony Robbins

Where B.O.G.E was about self confidence and the development of qualities that increase your chances of achieving your definition of success, L.O.G.E. is about confidence and the development of the skills you identify as increasing your chances of achieving your definition of success.. So what is the difference between qualities and skills? Qualities in this context would refer to soft skills. The biggest irony is that these are called 'soft', when in my opinion they are the most important, especially when it comes to success & happiness. Skills in this context refer to hard skills, which are skills that are tangible and a lot easier to measure. It's important to establish the difference between the two because it's very easy to confuse them. Just because you have the skills for a certain path, doesn't mean you have the qualities. E.g. Imagine you want to be an author, you might be able to type at 100 words per minute (a very useful skill for writing books) but you may hate discipline (which is paramount for writing a book). Most of the time people would solely identify whether or not they are good enough simply by the skills required. As I hope you can now see, doing so is only scratching the surface. It also touches on something very real...

JUST BECAUSE YOU ARE GOOD AT SOMETHING, DOESN'T MEAN YOU SHOULD DO IT

This is one of the many ways in which you can end up being swayed to pursue a path that doesn't give you true happiness and the feeling of success. There are multiple ways anyone can live their lives and I believe the purpose behind there being so many routes is so that you can find the right one for you. It's one of the true beauties of life. If we all had the same definition of success and happiness and we all pursued it, it would result in a lot of unhappiness for those who didn't make it. One of the first people that can push a person away from their true calling is their parents and family. I would argue that it is so easy to see yourself as not good enough just because you have been pursuing someone else's definition of success rather than your own. Many families have their own definitions of success that they then try to enforce onto their children. I myself come from an African heritage, where it is not uncommon for families to 'persuade' their children to pursue what is seen as high level professions (e.g. Accountant, Lawyer, Doctor, etc) and if a child shows any skills or potential to develop those skills relevant to those jobs, the attempts to 'persuade' can be even more intense. This can result in many children only doing things solely because their parents want them to, which can result in feelings of unfulfillment further down the line. This topic alone can be discussed in an entirely separate book but it is important to be aware of.

In school, maths was always my strongest subject, but I never liked it, whatsoever. If I pursued a career in maths I'm sure I would have been very successful financially speaking, but I would have been miserable.

In case you aren't too sure about Leaves of Good Enough. Here is a list of what I feel are the most important leaves of Good Enough a person needs to have and/or develop.

- **Competency:** To be able to execute required tasks to a valuable level in a timely manner
- **Assertiveness** - To establish, communicate and enforce internal & external boundaries
- **Communication:** To share your thoughts and feelings to others in a mutually beneficial way (Speaking & Writing), whilst receiving

and responding to others' thoughts and feelings in a mutually beneficial way (Listening and Reading)

- **Problem Solving:** To identify, anticipate and solve problems for
  yourself and/or others.
- **Persuasion** - To persuade others to share a belief and/or take an
  action that you propose

EXERCISE #15 - L.O.G.E ASSESSMENT [WB PG 33]

Let's start with competency. This is most appropriate to discuss when you
are at the part of your journey where you have been able to either identify
or confirm your definition of success (or at the very least a path that you
want to explore). Getting to this point was difficult for me, but competency
I feel is simpler, however not easy. This is the stage where you have the
qualities required to be good at something, but you simply don't know how
to do it. Once upon a time this was a difficult thing to address, but not anymore, due to the wonders of the internet (from Youtube, Wikipedia and
many others in between). So how can one discover what competency skills
you need in relation to your definition of success? Research, research and
more research (google is also your friend in this regard). This is often the
easiest to find because it's the most often spoken about. When it comes to
wealth (Work/Career/Business) you can find this by searching for job de-
scriptions and searching,

"How to ... "
"What skills do I need to be .... "

Doing this will give you a strong foundation of where to start. The issue
with this process however can be that you may have none or some of all the
skills that are needed. That being said, it's ok if you don't have them all. The

question is how do you feel about developing the other skills that you don't have? If you don't like the idea of developing them, then you should reassess whether or not there is another avenue you can walk through to your definition of success.

YOU NEED TO FEEL GOOD ABOUT THE JOURNEY TOO, NOT JUST THE DESTINATION(S)

The truth of the matter is that whatever you decide is your definition of success, you are going to be spending significantly more time in the journey than you are at the destination itself. If you decide to live your life based on an unenjoyable journey to a series of enjoyable destinations, you are setting yourself up for a far less fulfilling life. Ironically, the more you enjoy the journey, the more likely you are to reach the series of destinations.

EXERCISE #16 - COMPETENCY QUESTIONNAIRE [WB PG 34]

When you first started reading this section you may have thought the leaves of good enough were only concerning what I call competency (e.g. how to do a balance sheet as an accountant). The reality though is that competency is only one of many skills necessary. The simple reason why is because we quite simply aren't alone. As antisocial as you may feel you are (and I'm someone who absolutely loves my own company), humans are wired to operate better when they are with others. On top of that, us humans are wired to make decisions from a place of emotion rather than logic. Highly skilled sales people use this truth in the human condition to become good at their jobs. For the most part, the role of logic has been to justify, rationalise or address the emotion. Have you ever bought something that you knew you didn't actually need? I rest my case. And even if you have great control of your emotions, it doesn't mean that they don't have an influence on your decisions and your lifestyle choices.

Communication, problem solving and persuasion I will deal with in Reason 3. That being said, what matters is that you are aware of the other leaves and strive to work on your competency skills and assertiveness for you to feel good enough. This added with your branches and roots should have you feeling a lot better about yourself, as it did for me. The information on how you can cultivate the competency skills is so widespread online you can find it by accident. Alternatively you can ask someone you consider to already have the competency skills how they did it.

- 12 -

HOW TO DEAL WITH WEEDS (BOUNDARY MANAGEMENT)

"A weed is but an unloved flower"

Ella Wheeler Wilcox

How do weeds affect trees?

"Weeds do compete for moisture, nutrients and light; but they may also interfere with trees by releasing toxins, modifying soil and air temperatures and harbouring pests"

R J Davies

Working on your roots, branches and leaves of good enough can make you feel great about yourself. However, just like a tree can have strong roots, branches and leaves, all the work can be undone by weeds.

The nature of weeds is complex and consists of many layers, however what I must touch on at this stage is one of the best ways of dealing with the weeds... Assertiveness. To touch on this would be to bring back a conversation we started in the chapter on IPBs

ESTABLISH, COMMUNICATE, AND ENFORCE BOUNDARIES. TO YOURSELF, & ESPECIALLY TO OTHERS

If there is one thing that I would want anyone who reads this book to learn, it is how important it is to establish what you will and won't accept from yourself and others. This is vital because without this, life can push you around and whenever you feel life is doing that to you, it doesn't matter how much you have, you'll never feel happy OR successful. One of the biggest things that damage your self esteem, self confidence and confidence is the **inappropriate reaction towards a violation (either by yourself or others) of your internal and external boundaries**. My definition for inappropriate reaction is

A reaction that doesn't involve a consequence for the violation of the boundary

Other people can violate your boundary(s) without even knowing about it so the mere violation shouldn't knock you down, only not responding with the correct consequence is what will damage your tree of good enough.

When first coming across this truth I realised I have, on too many occasions, allowed others to violate my boundaries. But then again, I didn't even have established boundaries for myself and others to abide by, never mind the adequate consequences that I would enforce for each and every violation.

During my experience of tutoring, I came across a concept often called cause & consequence. Children I'd say from 8-12 can be the most challenging to teach (just my experienced opinion, but I'm open to the debate for those who disagree). Reason being is because maintaining control of the classroom is far more important than any information you have to teach them. On top of that children at that age are the most prolific when it comes to testing boundaries. You will need to go through a process of catching and enforcing each and every single violation before they acknowledge and abide by the boundaries. You can enforce a violation 9 times and if you don't appropriately enforce the 10th violation, you could lose the whole classroom and find it difficult to get them back in line. This is the same with life, especially if you haven't established boundaries before. Young people (similar to the rest of us) respond when they understand that there will be consequences for their actions (cause). Young people find it difficult to accept a consequence if they didn't feel warned about it ahead of time. Other times they won't accept it because they feel like the boundary shouldn't apply to them. And in this experience I learnt that you can identify people in three different categories when it comes to your boundaries

- Those who don't recognise your boundary(s)
- Those who recognise your boundary(s), but don't feel like it should apply to them
- Those who have issues with boundary(s) period

Each type of person needs a different response to deal with. There are more layers to the weeds but this will be addressed further in the next section. What is important is to know that all the work that you do on your Self Esteem, Self Confidence and Confidence can be undone.

Reason 4 also touches on another important factor to one's Tree of Good Enough; The Terrain. This should be seen as the weather where your tree is planted. An extreme example of this is planting a tree in a desert (you don't need an active imagination to sense the struggle that the average tree would have in growing in that environment)

The first step to dealing with weeds is to be aware they exist and commit to a lifestyle of looking for them and dealing with them swiftly, rather than letting them grow. Feeling and being good enough is a journey that doesn't end with you reading and finishing this section of the book. If anything, it's only the beginning....

GROUND ONE - HABITUALS

Before we move on to the other sections, here are the habituals for this section that have made a real difference for me

1. **Weekly Lookup**
   a. Review the following on a weekly basis
      i. Personal Bill of Rights
      ii. IPB Chart
      iii. Good Enough List
2. **Weekly R.O.G.E**
   a. Every week, name 1 situation where you displayed at least one of the qualities that you had listed as what qualifies you as good enough (you can do this as a written journal or even Voice notes)
3. **Weekly B.O.G.E.**
   a. Every week, name 1 situation where you used or demonstrated a quality that you consider important to your life/definition of success
4. **Weekly L.O.G.E.**
   a. Every week, name 1 situation where you used or demonstrated a competency skill that you consider important to your life/definition of success
5. **Gratitude Journal (Daily)**
   a. Every evening before bed, or morning after working up, write down 3 things that you are grateful for. It can be an experience, an outcome, an individual or group or anything in between
   b. Review them every 6 months

REASON TWO:
I DON'T FEEL LIKE I COULD HANDLE 'IT'

SIGNS & SYMPTOMS THAT YOU ARE SUFFERING FROM THIS INCLUDE, BUT ARE NOT LIMITED TO;

1. Feelings of Fear/Overwhelm/Anxiety
2. Procrastination/Escapism
3. Self-sabotage
4. Happiness/relief when people around you fail
5. Jealousy towards others around you, who you would consider successful

OBJECTIVE(S):

1. To understand the nature of one's 'It'
2. To overcome one's 'It'

My Truth

I'm easily overwhelmed and I simply haven't learned how to utilise fear. Even writing my truth on this matter is overwhelming. I have allowed fear to hold me back from being and doing what I've always felt deep down was truly for me, simply because I'm scared that I wouldn't be able to handle the outcome. The idea of trying my best at something and still failing fills me not only with dread, but despair. However bad things have gotten in my life, I've always felt like I had the potential to become successful. That being said, what if I become successful then lose it all? Mentally and emotionally, I don't think I could deal with that. If I were to get it and then lose it quickly, I'd rather have not had it at all.

My personal life experience has seen me in situations where soon after I achieved what I wanted and/or what made me happy, I would experience a feeling that I was soon going to lose it, or experience something negative enough to cancel out the positive accomplishment/achievement. This emotion would also be across my whole life, from career to even dating. It's gotten to the point where everything I consider important to me, I expect to lose. I have been raised in an environment where I experienced the feeling that risks were seen almost as if it was something that I couldn't or shouldn't take. I wouldn't be the first or last person who was raised in an overprotective household, with experiencing a lot of my childhood feeling like a lamb that was never meant to be strong enough to deal with the 'big bad' that is the world. My past and present inability to manage fear has manifested in me now being the person that puts everyone's thoughts, feelings and priorities ahead of mine.

"I don't mind taking the hit, if it means that no one else is hurt".

Another result of this inability to manage fear was the fact I saw everyone else's well being and how they felt about me as solely my responsibility. The risks that I did want to take, I simply didn't if I felt like it could cause the disapproval of those whose approval I sought. I also was scared to feel guilty for living my life and my truth, especially if it meant 'leaving behind' those same people - I desperately wanted to fit in and be accepted by these people, to the point where it directly affected my self esteem. The more approval I had, the greater the self esteem, and the more that approval was at threat, the greater I was frozen by fear. Who these people are doesn't matter as much as me emphasising the point that we all may experience this phenomenon of fear. However, as I've seen fear as nothing more than an anchor, there are people who have seen fear as fuel to propel them forward"

- 13 -
DISCOVERING YOUR 'IT'

"Fear kills more dreams than failure ever will"

Chris Dessi

The mind protects us from many things; one of the biggest things it protects us from are things that it thinks we cannot handle. Those things are determined by how we have responded to previous experiences and our perception of something, shaped by the opinions of people we hold a high opinion of.

The worse we respond to an experience, the stronger our mind will try to protect us from avoiding actions that it feels will increase the chance of that experience happening again. This can result in people not pursuing their definition of success, it did for me. If you believe going on a journey has the chance of you experiencing a situation you've previously encountered and reacted badly to, you'll most likely experience inner resistance.

This is the mind attempting to protect us from what it feels is a threat. The issue with this is that experiencing some things that we may feel threatened by is the only way we can get stronger. For example, some people avoid approaching someone they are attracted to because they have constantly experienced rejection (which they've taken badly) and assume it will happen again. Some avoid committing to a relationship because of how badly they have responded to the experience of being heartbroken from a previous relationship. Some people avoid being rich because they grew up in an environment where someone they held in high regard felt negatively about money (e.g. seeing money as the root of all evil), either as a result of their own experiences or someone else's that they hold in high regard. Attitudes and mindsets can be passed down from generation to generation.

I want to discern the difference between an experience, and your response to an experience. An experience is just that, an experience. Your response and/or your interpretation of that experience shapes what it is. I say this because two people can have the exact same experience but draw two different conclusions from it. This can then result in two different reactions to the same experience. The first person can interpret that experience as being the reason why they were never meant to become successful, whilst the second person can have the exact same experience and interpret that as confirmation that they <u>are</u> meant to be successful.

A small personal example of this is when I was a door-to-door fundraiser. It's a profession that is now effectively extinct but was truly something that wasn't for everyone. I would explain fundraising as a balance between sales and customer service, where resilience is the vital factor in the amount of new long term donors you can sign up. You can never really tell if someone will be a good fundraiser or not until they actually do it (or as we would call it 'going on the doors', such is the challenging nature of the profession. You can be as charismatic and articulate as you want. You can be the person who's always loved the idea of helping save lives. However, if 50+ people telling you no (oftentimes daily) affects you to the point that you expect no one to ever sign up, you are done for.

The most painful experiences of being told no weren't actually the rude ones (e.g. someone swearing at you, which didn't really happen to me but happened to many others I knew). The most painful experiences were when you either felt they were going to sign up or when you spent a lot of time with a potential donor trying to win them over. Those ones would hurt me the most because of the amount of energy and even emotion I would invest in them signing up. The more humans invest in something, the more they want to see a return on their investment (financially, mentally, physically, emotionally or even spiritually). Furthermore no one wants to leave something they feel they invested so much in, as it would often feel like their efforts were wasted. However, one of my mentors, by the name of Andy Grahn, shared with me a profound shift in perspective on how he would see the same experience. The closer he got to and missed a potential sign up, the more he was convinced that another one was coming very soon. I later realised that all the best fundraisers had this perspective. Not only that, but the best fundraisers often experienced the most rejection in comparison to the worst fundraisers. Why? Because the best fundraisers saw rejection as part of the game and doubled their attempts, whereas the worst fundraisers got rejected a handful of times and let it crush them. Some of the best fundraisers would even endeavour to compel potential donors to either sign up or give them a hard no.

So as you can conclude, the solution to this is to change your perspective (which we started in Reason One). However, I found for myself that to do this effectively, it is important to really get into what I feel I struggle to handle. Here is a non exhaustive list of some of the things that many people struggle to handle (myself included):

- Success
- Failure
- Being judged
- Being widely disliked
- Not meeting expectations, whether it be your own or of others (Internal or External)
- Embarrassment
- Guilt
- Shame

- Pressure
- Reality
- Accepting limitations
- Disappointing others
- Being Disappointed
- Disapproval
- Being betrayed/let down by someone close
- Being alone
- Abandonment
- The thought of dying
- Regrets
- Being a burden to others
- Change
- The unknown
- Loss
- Death

I've learned to acknowledge that there is a part of me that protects me from what it thinks I can't handle, or have shown in previous experience to struggle handling. I would say that not only could the actual experience be something that people can struggle to handle but also the 'idea' of that experience. For example, you may never have experienced what you consider failure, but the opinions of people around you can make you fear the idea of failure. Having a look at this list, I can automatically recall how all of these situations already triggered me into being convinced that I wasn't good enough. The funniest thing about this is that all of these things are situations that every human has already experienced or will experience. I have been through all of the above in this list and just being aware of that allowed me to gain real perspective on this reason as to why I'm not successful... yet. As you may soon realise, the more you go through this journey, the more you realise that you aren't the only one who has been in this same predicament.

EXERCISE #17 :'IT' LIST [WB PG 38]

When I did this exercise, I was surprised to realise that I actually reacted really well to a lot of the situations that were on the list. That being said, there were a good few occasions I reacted horribly to. What was a relief to know was that my thoughts of how I would react weren't completely aligned with how I have actually reacted in the past. At this stage I also appreciated that my 'It List' may well be surface level and that there was more work to do to truly have this handled. That's when I came up with my value...

VALUE #5: I CAN HANDLE 'IT'

The only solution to addressing this issue was learning how to handle 'It'. Everyone has things they are fearful of and I was naive enough to think that one can get to a point where they no longer have fear. I soon realised on this journey that there are people I would consider successful, who actually have experienced the same level, if not higher levels of fear than I have. They however used it to help them become successful. In comparison, I felt that this same fear is what has been holding me back, which has just been exposed as an excuse ... but we'll get to that one later.

As they say, the best way to handle fear is to confront it. Professionals would call this exposure therapy and this is a process of confronting your fear in stages to the point where you overcome it. The idea of confronting my fears that I actually reacted bad to was troubling enough, never mind actually doing it! So how would I be able to handle 'IT' if the idea of 'IT' still scares me?

The next thing I tried to do was meditate on the items of my 'IT' list being reality (five at a time, for one minute each item, per day). The idea behind this was the fact I was aware that many athletes would often mentally visualise themselves in high-level situations and being successful. I have done things like this before but at the same time, I think the reason why it wasn't as effective was because it didn't take into account my present reality. By that, I mean the hurdles that I face on a regular basis. More importantly, not only did I meditate, I made a point to notice how my body felt when I was going through these experiences, and I realised something profound.

THE WAY I BREATHED COMPLETELY CHANGED

For those of you who don't know, how a human breathes can greatly affect their health; physically, mentally, emotionally and also spiritually. A book can be written solely on breathing alone, and many have been (a recommendation of mine is Do - Breathe by Michael Townsend Williams). My breathing either became shallow or completely stopped; the more intense the emotions I was feeling during those 'IT' moments, the worse it was. What I decided to try was maintaining my breathing whilst imagining experiencing these moments. What do I mean by maintaining my breathing? Well the best method of breathing is through your diaphragm (imagine breathing through your stomach to help you do this). This is also called deep abdominal breathing and it is a great way to manage anxiety and any overwhelming emotion. The breathing I would do is breathing in deeply through the nose for 5 seconds and breathing out through the mouth for 5 seconds. I would do this breathing whilst continuing to imagine the items on my 'IT' list. The reason I wanted to try this is that I realised that I have to be comfortable dealing with all of life, not just the good bits. The very truth is ....

MY (AND QUITE PROBABLY YOURS) 'IT' LIST CONTAINED ITEMS THAT ARE GOING TO HAPPEN, REGARDLESS OF ONE'S ACTIONS

And if I'm scared of things that are going to happen at some point, it would make more sense to feel ok with being able to deal with it, rather than trying to avoid that truth.

EXERCISE #18 :'IT' MEDITATION [WB PG 40]

Doing this made me feel a lot more comfortable with not just my 'IT' list but life itself. The biggest takeaway from making this a habit was the simple fact that it was a great training method of dealing with fear. Whenever a fear would come up, I would do whatever I could to avoid the pain. From procrastinating, to hesitating to simply just freezing in the moment; as long as I didn't feel the emotion anymore then I had done my job. It also made me even more curious....

- 14 -

WHAT IS THE HEART OF YOUR 'IT'?

"Fear causes hesitation, and hesitation will
cause your worst fears to come true"

Patrick Swayze

I've spent some real time thinking about the answer to this question. After much soul searching, and in the most simple way I possibly can explain, I came to realise...

THE HEART OF 'IT' IS YOUR EXPECTATIONS AND ASSUMPTIONS

More specifically, it is the mismanagement of my expectations and assumptions. However, let's start with expectations...

Expectation: *A strong feeling that something will happen or be the case.*

In relation to expectations, I call this my 'Sense of Should'. I feel that everyone also has this sense of should, and it consists of expectations in the following categories.

Internal
1. What I feel I should already be doing (lifestyle)
2. What I feel should already have (possessions)
3. Who I feel should already be (identity)

External
1. The expectations people (whose approval/disapproval affects me) have of me

Any time that I didn't meet my expectations, I would feel like a failure and experience an immense sense of frustration. It took me a while to even realise that my continued sense of frustration came from not meeting my expectations. My biggest thought to myself would also be "I should have (Insert Accomplishment/Action/Outcome here) by now". But then again, do I even know what all of my expectations are? I then made a point to write them all down, across all parts of my life (health, wealth, personal growth, relationships & happiness).

EXERCISE #19 : INTERNAL 'SENSE OF SHOULD' QUESTIONNAIRE [WB PG 41]

I feel that because my Sense of Should is so far away from who I currently am, it's creating a conflict of sorts, within myself. I would imagine that a similar example to what I'm talking about is the stereotypical man's mid-life crisis. What makes this feeling more difficult is when I encounter experiences that highlight how far away I truly am, in comparison to my Sense of Should.

One of the other issues with my 'Sense of Should', is that it is too attached to external factors that I can't control (especially the expectations from others). The win for me was any experience where I acted as I felt I 'should' have. But I can't always control the outcome and having my self-confidence defined by external factors (which can be volatile) is unhealthy to say the least. When unearthing this truth, I felt inner resistance and I realised what may well be the heart of my 'IT'...

"FOR AS HARD AS YOU TRY, FOR AS LONG AS YOU TRY, YOU WILL NEVER BECOME THE PERSON AND HAVE THE LIFE YOU'VE ALWAYS WANTED. IT'S SIMPLY TOO LATE. AND EVEN IF YOU DID, YOU WOULD SOON LOSE IT ALL; WHILST WATCHING PEOPLE WHO AREN'T AS GOOD AS YOU (BUT WHO YOU HAVE HELPED) ACHIEVE SUCCESS"

This rocked me to my core when I first unearthed this truth of mine. I soon realised that my 'IT' statement from the previous chapter came from a dark place. A truthful, but dark place all the same. I asked myself why I felt this way and the biggest thought that would pop up would be;

"IF IT WAS GOING TO HAPPEN, IT WOULD HAVE HAPPENED BY NOW!"

I have always had this fantasy of being successful by an early age. I also felt that If I became successful later on in life, that somehow wouldn't mean as much. For those of you who currently share this same belief I want to share with you a story. I remember being 17 and Suna (a man I consider a mentor and continue to look up to) once asked me whether I would want a Range Rover at 25 or 45 years of age.

I immediately said 25 without question. It wasn't even a debate to me. He laughed at me (which I was confused about). He then went on to explain why 45 will always be the better option. With getting a Range Rover at 25 years of age, you are most likely not going to have the same level of appreciation for the car as you would if you were 45. On top of that, your perspective at 25 is far more naive than when you are 45. Getting something later greatly increases your chances of being able to keep it. A great example of this is the fact that he asked me how much I thought a Range Rover was. I quickly searched for the price of the most recent Range Rover at the time and hit him back with the number, which I believe was around £50,000 (but don't quote me). He then laughed and explained that just because I could afford the money for buying the car, doesn't mean that I could afford to run the car. As many of you who have cars will know, owning a car is much more complex than just being able to afford the price of the car itself; from insurance, to fuel, to repairs if and when the car breaks down (never mind maintenance costs to reduce the chances of it breaking down).

All of these costs quickly tell you whether or not you can truly afford something. At 45, those other costs are far less of an issue. Just remembering this story reminds me of the simple fact that this thought I had in my head wasn't only incorrect, it was baseless. As I am older, I can now say that I'd be far better equipped to keep that Range Rover longer when I reach 45 than I would have ever been able to at 25.

On a similar tangent, society is filled with stories of successful people that achieved success when they were older. Here is a few who either started their journey or actually became 'successful' at these ages:

- Vera Wang - 40
- Stan Lee (Marvel Comics) - 39
- Samuel L Jackson - 43
- Ray Croc (McDonalds) - 52
- Oprah Winfrey - 32

If I were to achieve even a fraction of what the people in this list did, I would be very happy. On top of that it would seem somewhat of a fair trade to achieve those things, but do it at that age. Having irrefutable evidence that my thinking wasn't actually a fact, I realised the same thing about my 'IT'.

'IT' WAS AN ASSUMPTION!!!!! (TO BE CONTINUED)...

- 15 -
LIGHT & DARK: LET'S TALK

"The place where Light and Dark begin to touch is where miracles arise"
Robert A Johnson

Professor Khonsu (author of Sacred Man) once told me that all thoughts, emotions and behaviours come from two core emotions; Love & Fear. It was one of the most profound things I've ever heard and it triggered the path I've taken to better understand this dynamic. Many mediums, from TV to social media, would speak on topics of how to exorcise your demons or cast dark aside from your life - but what if they were always meant to work in tandem? In this context, the Light is your **spirit** and the Dark is your **mind.** I've since realised how important it is to understand both your Light & Dark and manage the relationships with both, so that they can both support you in your definition of success, as well as making the world a better place.

Your spirit is the part of you that wants you to be successful, the eternal optimist and dreamer. Your mind is the pragmatist, the person that remembers everything that has happened to you and believes what you can and can't do, based on what's already happened.

Seeing your spirit and your mind this may make you feel like it's a winner takes all battle.. The goal isn't to fight it out amongst each other however, but to get the two to work in harmony. Why might you ask? Because I truly believe that the true goal of life is balance. Nature works very much on this concept and when things are out of balance is when you see unnatural instances in the world.

Your mind behaves like a separate person and just like any person, it is driven by self-preservation. It's the reason why it resists desires from your spirit. The mind is often a manifestation of all the things you've been through, as well as all the people you've experienced and how you reacted to those things. Your spirit on the other hand is a gift from God (or the universe if you are not religious). This spirit I feel is your north star as to what will make YOU happy and it's the part of you that you tap into when you are trying to discover and accept your definition of success (also known as your higher self in other circles).

The spirit is resolute, whereas the mind can be easily swayed. The question you have to ask is what part of you do you listen to the most? What you may have already realised is that the previous chapters of this book were designed to help you cultivate one's Light. I feel that one of the key reasons why I am not successful...yet, and many others aren't either is because of the faulty way in which we interpret the things that have happened to us in our lives, suppressing our Light. We often either experience ourselves or those who we hold in high regard, dismiss our Light (what we've genuinely wanted to do). We allow life and people in our lives to cast doubt and scepticism over our true dreams. Why?

THE VAST MAJORITY OF HUMANS HAVE NOT ACCOMPLISHED THEIR OWN DREAMS

It is important to understand this because this is just another step in gaining perspective in the fact that your own thoughts and emotions may well have been influenced by these types of people. I mentioned the 'Terrain' earlier in this book and will later reference how this concept relates to one's Light and Dark and how dealing with this greatly helped me, but I want to continue to focus on the internal Light and Dark. If you have read this book from the beginning, not only would you have understood how I cultivated my own Light, you may have done the exercises and cultivated your own Light. During that time, you may have experienced a part of yourself pushing back against the work you were doing. I most definitely experienced this and this is the reason why I wanted to cultivate my Light before dealing with the Dark. If you want to get rid of the dark in your house, you turn the light on.

I also realised that my 'IT' became a lot easier to identify when I took the time to truly define what success was to me, as well as working to improve my self-esteem, self-confidence and confidence. The problem I experienced with only working on cultivating my Light, was feeling that success meant no presence of the Dark whatsoever. During this time however, I would continue to experience the Dark. What makes the Dark so powerful is that it is fuelled by real experiences that I have had in my lifetime, especially my childhood. The Dark is quite simply something that can't and shouldn't be ignored. I didn't realise that I was already working on better understanding my Dark by doing the previously mentioned exercises in this section of the book. In case you weren't sure as to the reason why I feel it is important to deal with both Light & Dark, it is because…

LIGHT AND DARK HAS BEEN & WILL FOREVER BE A PART OF YOUR LIFE

As a facetious example, imagine trying to live the rest of your life based on the belief that if even one drop of rain touches your skin, you'll die. How would you live? It would be absolutely ridiculous to try and you'd probably never leave your house, and even if you did you would be overly cautious and would probably lose a lot of enjoyment from your life (special exceptions for those who have a genuine allergic reaction to rain, but I'm sure you understand the point I'm getting at). So let's address the elephant in the room and get straight to it.

So what's the solution to addressing this problem? The first step is self-talk/internal dialogue. It has been said that humans have over 60,000 thoughts a day (which is ridiculous to think about, pardon the pun). I simply had to learn how to monitor and change the dynamic of my internal dialogue. One thing that I had noticed is that the clearer my goals and plans were, the stronger my inner resistance (or my Dark, whichever way you prefer to see it). Therefore, I tried dealing with it head on and giving the Dark "permission" to speak its own mind. Before I could start a conversation with my Dark however, I had to become more aware of the thoughts that were coming from this place. The first thing I wanted to do is ask this part of myself some questions and just listen to its answers.

EXERCISE #20: 'WHY NOT?' QUESTIONNAIRE [WB PG 44]

Listening to the Dark, I realised that all it was doing was reflecting memories of experiences that I reacted strongly to. From this point on, I'm going to refer to the Dark as simply the mind. The reason why is because I realised during this journey that the mind was designed to help a human with their endeavours. I realised that I unfortunately didn't cultivate a healthy relationship between myself and my mind. A big part of that came from the fact that I previously thought that myself and my mind were one of the same. However, just like my thoughts, emotions, and actions are not myself - neither is my mind. Take the example of a house, my mind might be a bedroom in my house, but my bedroom isn't my whole house, just a part of it. With all that being said, I had to be able to realise and manage all of the things that were a *part* of me, rather than seeing them as me. Thus, the birth of my next value came...

VALUE #6: 10:90

10:90 is referring to the fact that 10% of your life is what has happened to you and what will happen to you; the 90% of your life is **how you respond**

to those things (I alluded to this at the end of the previous chapter, it was only later I came up with number ratio as an easier way to remember the value). I didn't realise how much of my life I blamed on my circumstances. This value alone doesn't really do much, so I wanted to create some exercises to help me honour that value. The first step was to learn to have conversations with my mind and use my spirit to help the two work in tandem. What helped me start this was the value I came up with whilst working on my self-esteem; for those of you don't remember, it was...

EVERYTHING THAT HAPPENS TO ME IS DESIGNED TO HELP ME ACHIEVE MY DEFINITION OF SUCCESS, BUT IT'S FOR ME TO FIGURE OUT HOW

The challenge to get the spirit and the mind working together starts here and will bleed into the next section (Reason 4). This challenge started with me having a conversation with two parts of myself, my mind and my spirit. I imagined that both were different characters in a TV show live debate, where they would try and persuade each other of their prospective positions. It took a while to really feel comfortable with this so don't feel bad if you give this a go and find it challenging. Be patient, and your answers will come in time. What also helped me was having the conversation in reference to goals I had always wanted to achieve. It was from the perspective of both asking the question "So what do you think of your possibility of achieving this goal?" From asking that question, I could feel both my mind and spirit ready to communicate and easier to listen to.

EXERCISE #21: LIGHT VS DARK CONVO [WB PG 47]

From doing this exercise, I realised that I had previously seen my mind as the enemy, when it can actually be one of my strongest allies in helping me achieve my definition of success. Michael E Gerber (in his book E-Myth) touches on the concept of the entrepreneur and the manager. The entrepreneur is the person who comes up with the vision and the manager is the person that is not necessarily a visionary, but knows how to make things happen. He further makes the point that businesses benefit from having both in an organisation. My spirit and mind can work in the same way, where my spirit is the entrepreneur with the creative vision and my mind being the vessel to help make it a reality. I also understand that this conversation between myself, my spirit and my mind will not only be a constant conversation for the rest of my life, but it's one that I actually look forward to. I don't see brushing my teeth twice a day for the rest of my life as a prison sentence, so why should I see it as such when it comes to personal growth and development? (especially when I benefit from both of them). If there is one point that I want to emphasise is simply that internal dialogue is a part of all of our lives, whether we like it or not. As such, if it's going to continue until we die, why not take ownership and control of the conversation?

- 16 -

THE VICTIM VS THE HERO: WHICH ONE DO YOU WANT TO BE?

"Who lives inside your head? The Hero of your story,
or the Victim of someone else's"

Tony Curl

As I got better at my internal dialogue, I recognised that humans not only enjoy hearing stories but also telling stories (to themselves as well as others). The stories I'm referring to are the stories that we can end up telling ourselves to explain where we are and why. I started realising that I would often identify myself as the victim of my own story. Whenever certain situations would happen, one of the first thoughts that would come up would be that the situation was confirmation or a repeat of the story that I was telling myself. This story (and the stories within it) were behind all of the problems that I have so far identified as being the reasons why I'm not successful… yet. These stories have made me feel safe, but deeper than that, these stories have made it easier for me to deal with the pain of not meeting my own expectations.

Like myself, I feel many others (without realising it) identify themselves as the victim in their own story, and with this comes the biggest impediment to their own growth...blame. Blaming others can be comforting to the soul, but only in the short term. In my case, being comforting in the short term is exactly what I needed. The problem with the short term in general is that what may feel good in the short term often tends to make a situation worse in the long term. A great example of this is food. The best tasting food in the short term is often the processed, unhealthy food, heavy in sugar, salt, fat or all three. The result will often be the food having greater taste than the healthier alternatives. However whilst the food high in sugar, salt and fat will greatly affect you long term, the healthier foods (which don't taste anywhere near as good to most of us) will help you in the long term. In modern western society, the majority of us have prioritised taste, price and convenience (short term) over long-term health benefits.

Blame and responsibility have been treated the same way. I've had to accept that I've prioritised the convenient, short term gratification and comfort of blame over the long term, uncomfortable and inconvenience of taking responsibility. I've gotten much better over the years with taking responsibility. I realised that what was holding me was still blaming others in areas where I could really grow if I took responsibility for that also. What really helped me with this was to examine how much blame I still place on others and to what degree do I still feel like it's affecting me currently.

EXERCISE #22: VICTIM STORY [WB PG 50]

I felt really good after writing out my story. I also realised how easy it is to blame others for any and every part of our lives. It made me realise how easy it is to be okay with not being successful due to things not being in our control going against us. Yes, I have my Sense of Should, but if external things that I can't control were powerful enough to stop me, it made it easier to deal with me not being where I should be. The issue though, is that my perspective is out of whack. The win for me previously was any experience where the outcome was what I 'felt' it should be. However, I can't always control the outcome and having my self-confidence defined by external factors (which can be volatile) is unhealthy. What I've realised is that the real win is any experience where...

OPPORTUNITIES TO LEARN AND GROW ARE IDENTIFIED, WHILST ENJOYING THE IDEA OF TRYING AGAIN

Blaming others robs me of the opportunity to learn and grow. Of course, external factors are important, but not as important as I had previously thought. External factors should only be used to sharpen one's focus in improving the internal factors. As stated previously, true maturity is when you realise what you can and can't control, whilst embracing responsibility for the former and avoiding blaming others for the latter. I thought the things I couldn't control were always more powerful than the things I could control. The biggest thing that isn't said though is that the things that you can control are so powerful, it is more than enough for you to be truly happy and successful.

Generally speaking, what can one control? Here's a short list to start with...

- The present moment
- Their breathing
- Their reactions
- Time spent on something
- How many times they try

Here are some great books I recommend for helping one learn how to maximise the effectiveness of what they can control

1. Do Breathe: Calm Your Mind. Find Focus. Get Stuff Done - Michael Townsend Williams
2. Practicing The Power of Now - Eckhart Tolle
3. Time Warrior - Steve Chandler
4. War of Art - Steven Pressfield

Let's be clear, there are some books that should be read once and there are some that should be read on a regular basis (whether it's every 6 months or every year, etc). These four books I'd include in the latter category and all of these elements I've used to better understand how I can be the hero of my own story.

EXERCISE #23: HERO STORY [WB PG 54]

Note: In a true story, you will know that there are villains as well as victims and heroes. That is something that I will address in the next section of the book.

The idea of becoming the hero in my story made me a lot less fearful about going for what I want in life. Of course, fear will forever be a part of all of our lives and I can appreciate that I was previously dealing with fear with the intention of getting rid of it forever. This has led to the frustration that I feel when it continues to come back in waves in holding me back from achieving my definition of success. But not only was I already a superhero, I also had super powers that can be mastered to get what I wanted out of life. The more I understood this truth the less scary the things I can't control were.

In conclusion, I've managed to start the conversation with myself in helping address the feeling that I couldn't handle 'IT' but I felt like there was more work to be done to address this and make it part of my reality. The next step was therefore to start creating processes that will help me to achieve my definition of success. I then realised that the 'process' also would help with my fear of being able to handle 'IT', in the sense that....

THE PROCESS IS DESIGNED NOT JUST TO HELP YOU GET TO YOUR DEFINITION OF SUCCESS, BUT TO GET YOU READY TO HANDLE IT WHEN IT COMES

My perspective changed from seeing my fears as an obstacle to seeing them as sparring partners and allies. But what is the process…?

GROUND TWO – HABITUALS

1. **'IT' List** - Review weekly (also add to/take away from it when necessary)
2. **'IT' List Meditation** - Meditate Daily on at least 5 items of your (1 minute per item)
3. **Light vs Dark Convo** - Pick a goal you want to achieve in the week and have conversation from both sides each week
4. **Victim Story** - Write your victim story out whenever you feel like a victim, either in a specific situation or generally
5. **Hero Story** - Write every week (keep it specific to what has happened to you in that week and how you will respond)

REASON THREE:

I HAVE TRUST ISSUES
(ESPECIALLY WITH OTHER PEOPLE)

SIGNS & SYMPTOMS THAT YOU ARE SUFFERING FROM THIS INCLUDE, BUT ARE NOT LIMITED TO;

1. You try to do everything yourself
2. You struggle with asking others for help
3. You feel "If you want a job done properly, do it yourself"
4. Perfectionism
5. You won't take on projects/tasks that will require help from someone else.
6. Isolation
7. Asking for help at the last minute

OBJECTIVE(S):

1. To understand the value that other people can add to aid one's achievement of their definition of success/happiness
2. To understand the power of one's 'pillars of people'
3. To learn how to manifest the power of people and their pillar

My Truth

This is without a shadow of a doubt the most difficult reason for me to address. Funnily enough, the discovery of the other four reasons mentioned in this book came from me trying to address this problem. For as long as I can remember, I've associated success with being able to do things without anyone else's help. The more you can do things by yourself, the smarter and more successful you are perceived as, right? I also associated asking for help and working with others as a sign of weakness. On top of that, my childhood led me to one of many simple conclusions: people aren't to be trusted.

Both my parents are business people in their own right, and I was exposed to two different ways of doing things. I saw my mum be the 'Do Everything Yourself' person, who would do things by herself, refuse help most of the time and whenever she finally would allow someone to help her, quickly do the task herself or re-do the work someone else had done for her. I also noticed how she wouldn't really trust people. The only person that I felt she trusted and has ever trusted since, was my late older brother (who passed away at 15, when I was 7)

My Dad on the other hand was more of the 'Manager', where he would have everyone else get things done. It almost looked like he was 'Do Nothing Yourself', as it didn't look like he did anything but was always recognised as the boss. Not only that, it felt like he trusted other people all too easily. I feel that our opinions on things are linked to our emotions towards others, especially parents. For example, the unresolved relationship between myself and my Dad was for a long time the reason I severely disliked glasses and business suits (which he religiously wore), never mind his business management style.

Because my Mum played more of a prevalent presence in my life versus my father, I can accept that I've taken on a lot of her patterns of behaviour and her perspective towards business. Without getting into specifics (which may well be spoken about in another book, and after I have a private conversation with my Dad) I feel that my lack of trust in others can be linked to my lack of trust in my Dad, from living a childhood of continued broken promises. Broken promises may be bad enough but my Dad could make you feel like he was Martin Luther King, but the continued lack of follow through may well have been one of the factors in me struggling to trust others.

Whenever I am in a situation where I consider asking someone else for something, I feel convinced of the following...
- The person will probably say no to doing it
- If the person actually says yes, they probably won't end up doing it at all
- If the person actually decides to do it, they won't do it to a good enough level
- If the person actually decides to do, they won't do it as well as I could do it
- This person will only do it for themselves, rather than doing it for me.

And my conclusion to this thought process has often been...

"Why bother asking?, I already know how it's going to turn out, and I can always trust myself more than anyone else"

I also took a lot of pride in being able to do things by myself. I even felt sorry for those in school who always had to ask for help. As I got older I even took pride in being the person that people would come to for help and advice. I truly felt that I was beyond ever needing help or advice from others.

I've always felt a lot more comfortable doing tasks on my own, by myself, rather than with others, in front of others. I often felt slowed and weighed down by having to deal with others and I felt that I was at my best whenever I would remove myself from the presence of others and do it all on my own. If I wanted to do something that would be too big to do by myself, I'd either try to do it by myself anyway, or rationalise that the task wasn't worth completing in the first place and move on to do something else. The idea of working on something that would leave me exposed if someone I've asked for help doesn't deliver, fills me with enough anxiety to feel claustrophobic.

Even though I've put this as the second to last reason, I would argue that nothing else would change without me addressing this reason. Trust issues doesn't just mean trusting others, it also ties in to not being able to trust yourself. I say that because the people that I would consider the most successful are often not only helped by others, they PROACTIVELY ask others for help, whether they can do the task themselves or not. This is why this is Reason 3 and not Reason 1. As important as relationships are with others, working to resolve this reason unearthed the other reasons which had to be addressed so that I could truly address this one. Reasons 0-2 are reasons that I solely have control over and addressing them will build a greater foundation with dealing with the last two Reasons. From this I realised that I didn't even trust myself and thus it would be nigh on impossible to trust others if I don't trust myself first.

Throughout my childhood, I witnessed and experienced asking for help as a sign that you couldn't do something, which was heavily implied as a weakness. The less I need to ask for help, the better human being I saw myself, and the more accomplished. I also took pride in the fact that I didn't seem to need as much help as other people around me to do something (a mistake I must admit). Thus soon became my definition of success; being able to do amazing things without anyone's help. The millionaire/billionaire I wanted to be was the 'self-made' one. Being a millionaire/billionaire but not 'self-made' was like cheating and not worth the accomplishment, so I thought. If I'm honest, one thing I've realised about one of the foundations behind this belief was the fact that deep down, I felt that the only way I would be noticed or appreciated by the world would be if I was alone.

I also hated the idea of being vulnerable in front of others. I always wanted to be the person who looked like they had everything together. I'd be more than happy to comfort someone in their time of need, but I would never allow myself to even be seen as needing comfort. So how do I address this reason? The short answer I realised was to let go of my past trauma/hurt and to manifest the power of people. The following chapters in this section are about doing just that.

- 17 -
WHO HURT YOU?

"You will know that forgiveness has begun when you recall those who hurt you and wish them well"

Lewis B Smedes

When resolving to tackle this issue head on, I eventually realised that before any action or habit or routine was to become a permanent fixture in my life. I had to confront the proverbial elephant in the room. If you read the previous section (Reason 2: I Don't Feel Like I Can Handle 'IT') you would have read the chapter that touches on writing a victim story. And if you have done the exercise, you may think that they are touching on the same thing as this chapter. You would be right, but also wrong. The victim story is about who you **blame** for where and who you are, whereas this section is touching on **everyone who hurt you and to what extent.**

The reason it is important to make this distinction is because the blame game is a game of broad strokes. However, looking into who hurt you can allow you to scan through and identify the smallest bit of residue of hurt that compounded into this greater overall emotion. This is the case for me. I can't hope to heal from my trust issues without going through ALL of the people that have hurt me in my life and the extent in which it went to. Without confronting that, my trust issues will continue to rear its ugly head. This is vital because as we desire to change and/or grow as humans, opportunities to grow and change will present themselves. Whether that would be in the form of other people presenting them to us (particularly strangers) or a possible job promotion, investment opportunities, a community project and anything else you can think of. The problem was that my trust issues made it difficult to recognise a good opportunity to grow as just that. I was more likely to see this kind of opportunity as another avenue to be betrayed, let down, disappointed, and the ultimate consequence; even more jaded and less likely to trust again. I believe that because us humans are wired to function better when we work together rather than alone, we are also wired to desire to trust others. But as life circumstances may condition us to not trust, we innately suffer, as we are suppressing our true nature. This isn't designed to make your experiences and your subsequent reasons not to trust any less valid. It's more about confronting those experiences and changing one's perspective on trusting others.

The first step though is identifying who hurt you and to what extent. The questions I asked myself during this was the following:

1. Who hurt me?
2. How did they hurt me?
3. What effect did it have on me?
4. When did they hurt me?
5. What was their motive?

Let's focus on the first three questions...,

EXERCISE #24: HURT LIST [WB PG 60]

How many people were on your list? Doing this made me realise that my list of who hurt me was deeper than I had previously thought. To really go through my list I had to uncomfortably go back in time. From birth, to primary and secondary school, to College and University, to when I first started working and everything in between. I was shocked at how much past hurt and trauma had compounded into the manifestation that is my trust issues (many of which I completely forgot about). What made this process even more profound was that I found myself mentally stuck in those moments. Regardless of the progress I made as a person, I deep down felt that I would still be the victim to those people, now and forever. Now the purpose of this isn't to wallow in past trauma and hurt (which may feel very easy to do). So what is the next step? The next step is to address the final two questions, but to go deeper by doing the following...

1. Try to contemplate their motive(s)
2. Forgive & Let It Go
3. Let It Go & Forgive
4. Forgive or Let It Go

It is a lot easier to contemplate forgiving someone if they already knew that they hurt you and expressed deep remorse, however...

IT IS POSSIBLE THAT THE PEOPLE WHO HURT YOU EITHER DON'T KNOW, DON'T REMEMBER OR DON'T CARE THAT THEY HURT YOU AND/OR TO WHAT DEGREE

Not forgiving someone and deciding to not let things go is like swallowing a poisoned pill and hoping your enemy dies from it. Many have distorted the idea of forgiveness. It may be easy to feel like forgiving someone is about that person and doing them the favour, when really it is about yourself and doing yourself the favour. If you don't forgive, you'll end up stuck in time and struggling to move on. In a circumstance when the very people who hurt you have moved on, you would probably become angrier and more bitter. One final profound thing about this is that whoever may have deeply affected you and your life story may not have even been a footnote in their own life story. There are always three sides to every story; how you remember it, how the other person remembers it and the truth. And I had to make the painful realisation...

YOUR TRUST ISSUES ARE QUITE POSSIBLY WORSENED BY THE FACT THAT YOU ONLY EVER CONSIDERED YOUR POINT OF VIEW

This is not about making excuses for the person/people that have hurt you. This is about the fact that considering all sides may not only make it an easier pill to swallow, but this will make it easier for you to forgive them, which **only benefits you**.

In addition to this, forgiveness can be difficult because we may feel like we are in some way dishonouring the past versions of ourselves (as well as possibly others close to us) who were hurt, and forgiving those who hurt us would be not handing out the deserving punishment to the person(s) responsible. Now let's tackle those final two questions

EXERCISE #25: FORGIVENESS LETTERS [WB PG 63]

NB: If you were anything like me. Your hurt came through in waves and this may be an exercise that you have to do on more than one occasion to truly get over the hurt. Please do this as many times as you feel adds value to you. A good idea is to do it once a month for anyone you are finding it difficult to forgive, but the choice is yours.

I'll only speak for myself and say that this was one of the most difficult exercises for me to do in this journey. From doing this, I realised how comforting it felt to hold onto the anger, pain and all the other negative emotions I had towards the people that were on my hurt list. As I was going through this process I could feel myself letting go of those emotions that were once comforting, but were actually holding me back. Whilst thinking about all the people that I have felt wronged me, I realised that there are two sides to a coin and a question came into my mind soon after....

WHO HAVE I HURT?

123

- 18 -
WHAT IF YOU'RE A VILLAIN?

"People are hero for some, victim for some and villain for some.
It's only a matter of perspective"

Ayan Dragneel Sinha

Whilst doing the work from the perspective that I was the victim but I had the power to be the hero, it dawned on me that I could also be the villain in someone else's story. The key that I realised in building relationships and working on my trust issues with people was empathy and being able to comprehend how things have been for other people. When I thought of how I could do this, I couldn't think of a better way than to think of how things have been for other people in relation to me. It then hit me that there might be a correlation between lack of trust in others and the actions one has taken towards others. A crass example of this is someone who is being unfaithful to their romantic partner, but as a result of this has trust issues concerning their own partners' fidelity.

True relationships are based on each person being able to hold themselves accountable. I noticed how in relationships, humans can often blame the other person for the problem(s) rather than asking themselves if they should also be held accountable. I'd like to think that I'm not a villain in anyone's story, but I have to be prepared to truly examine this part of my life, especially if it can help me address this issue.

The people who would see you as a villain would be those who felt they were treated badly by you or because of you. Here is a list of people I would argue may see you as the villain in their story

- Siblings (due to actions you took towards them)
- Siblings (e.g. due to your preferential treatment from your parents)
- Parents
- Ex boyfriends/girlfriends/Husbands/Wives
- Ex Friends
- Enemies
- Coworkers you either dislike, or dislike you
- Employees/subordinates who feel slighted
- Fans and or supporters (if you are a celebrity, public figure or someone of great influence)

EXERCISE #26: VILLAIN LIST [WB PG 73]

Before doing this exercise, I didn't see myself as a villain in other people's stories. Big mistake. There were more people on the list than I thought there would be. This actually prompted me to reach out to some of them and apologise (the ones that were in my immediate vicinity) and I truly implore you to do the same. Life is a lot more fulfilling when you are pre-pared to do the same things for others that you would want others to do for you. That's true maturity, and an even higher level of maturity is you having to do those things first. I truly believe in the old adage that you reap what you sow. What you receive truly is a reflection of what you put into the uni-verse. You can't expect or receive what you are not prepared to give. The issue is some people believe that they should reap directly from where they've sowed. A great example of this is when you help a particular some-one (let's call them James) and expect them to return the favour. Often that may not happen, but what is more likely to happen is that someone else (let's call them Mary) helps you. In this example, Mary may not have ever known you before she decided to help you. The greatest film that illustrates my philosophy on this is a film called Pay It Forward (2000). I strongly urge you to watch it. With that being said...

EXERCISE #27: APOLOGY LETTER [WB PG 76]

Funnily enough, the people I reached out to were perfectly ok, didn't hold it against me and deemed it a non issue. I felt a lot better about it and this eased a lot of the guilt that I didn't realise I was holding onto. With that being said, forgiveness is not something you should ever pressure people into. It is and will forever be their choice, and their choice only. All you can do is apologise and ask them for forgiveness. Another factor I didn't realise…

HOW YOU INTERPRET SOMETHING
MAY NOT ACTUALLY BE THE TRUTH

Self-forgiveness is more important than the forgiveness of others. On the surface, it might come across as selfish, but it's more important because without self-forgiveness, forgiveness from others won't mean anything to you (but it will help them). It's important though to take accountability for the things you have done to others, because it makes the process of you apologising to and asking them for forgiveness, whilst forgiving yourself, a lot more complete of a process. How would you be able to know all of the things to apologise to and forgive yourself for if you haven't taken into account ALL of the things to be apologetic about?

EXERCISE #28: SELF FORGIVENESS LETTER [WB PG 78]

Doing this truly confirmed to me that a massive part of my trust issues with others was my trust issues within myself. As I went through all of my life experiences of hurt, I realised that I had made a subconscious conclusion. For my own protection, it was better to live a life where I didn't have to rely on anyone else but myself. People were only there to disappoint and I often

126

take disappointment badly, therefore it would be foolish to live a life where other people were necessary if it would lead to more disappointment. Of course my spirit was in conflict with this notion, as I (like any other human) desire social interaction, whether that is with friends, family or of the romantic kind. The potential harm of others I considered more of a reality than their potential added benefit . I didn't want to believe that I had other people supporting me to then realise that I was alone anyway. If we are truly alone, I'd rather not indulge in the 'illusion' of being supported to then be exposed to 'reality'. I'd rather just stay 'alone' compared to feeling supported and then abandoned. College was a weird time, where I felt like a welcomed guest everywhere I went, but I didn't feel a sense of belonging anywhere.

I felt I was more tolerated than embraced or welcomed. Whether that was college, or even at the studio when I was trying to be a music producer. I would want to do all these different events and do different things in life and would often ask people if they wanted to go, and the response from many was very wishy washy. Rather than stop myself from doing the things that I wanted to do because no one wanted to do it with me, I started going to places and doing things by myself. I grew a lot more in self confidence because of this, but also as a result, I began to enjoy my own company too much and didn't feel like I really needed people anymore. I had got to a point where I could make myself happy and didn't really have a group of friends like other people. Rather than having one group of friends I would end up having many different groups of friends from many different walks of life. I could be at an event and be the only person I know at the beginning of it, then walk away knowing people from all different parts of life and the world. I took pride in the notion of being a lone wolf. Everything I had achieved I had managed to do myself, when it came to dating, I didn't have or need anyone else to set me up with someone. I created my own opportunities in life and took pride in the fact that no one person could say that without them I was nothing. But at the same time, thinking about the people that I've hurt made me realise that life isn't one sided. We all have the same capacity to be hurt by others, as we do to hurt others. So having made peace with this fact and thinking about how I was previously living my life, I then asked myself...

WHAT HAVE YOU EVER ACHIEVED ALONE?

"Great things in business are never done by one person"

Steve Jobs

"It is amazing what you can accomplish if you do not care who gets the credit"

Harry S Truman

Having been previously hurt in moments where I trusted others, it was important to remind myself of the benefits of trusting others. The experiences we have had can be so painful that we can convince ourselves that there is no benefit to trusting others.

When I realised and accepted that my trust issues may well be one of the biggest reasons I am not successful...yet, I had to ask myself the same question that is the name of this chapter. The funny thing however is that there is literally nothing that I have ever achieved by myself. This took me a very long time to reconcile. What hasn't helped is the absolute societal fallacy which is known as being 'Self-Made'. I was obsessed with being a self-made millionaire. It just had a certain ring to it and whenever I would watch a documentary or something on TV that would chronicle the story of someone who was 'self-made' it always inspired me. As a result, I saw being able to achieve something alone as a true sign of being special and a symbol of excellence. Growing up, I had interpreted the notion of receiving help as for people who simply weren't good enough. And as a result, whenever I felt like I 'might' need help, I would feel shame and guilt. This manifested in me doing all I could to do everything by myself even if it came at a cost to my well being. To truly get started on manifesting the power of people, I would have to dismantle the notion that I can and have already done things by myself. Yes you can achieve something without the present help of someone, but at the same time you have been helped by something someone created or has done in the past, these include but are not limited to...

- Technology/Inventions (created by others)
- Education (mainstream/self study) (provided by others)
- Medication (created by others)

Even things that you can do with your body, like clench your fist, can be done due to the simple fact that your mother and father conceived, gave birth and nurtured you to the point where your hand is healthy enough to do it.

EXERCISE #29: 'SELF MADE' STRESS TEST [WB PG 81]

Not only did I realise that the concept of self-made was BS, but it also goes against human nature. There is a reason why isolation can cause illnesses such as depression, stroke, and increased risk of heart disease. What is even more profound was not only am I not self made, but I wasn't previously aware of how many people have helped me to achieve what I have so far, especially the achievements that I consider most important to me.

One of the things I love doing as a pastime is to have conversations with others and ask them what they have ever managed to do by themselves, here is a conversation I had with someone a while ago...

"But I have done things all by myself"

"Ok, name me one thing that you've done by yourself"

"I wrote a poem all by myself without any help from anyone"

"Ok, what did you use to write it with"

"I used my phone"

"OK, did you build the phone by yourself?
The same phone that allowed you to write the poem?"

"hmmmm"...

I didn't relay this conversation to be facetious, but more to highlight the point that society has misled itself with the word self-made and us humans not only need help from each other, but actually thrive from it. The most successful people I know didn't just get offered help from others, but rather they would go out of their way to invite others to help them. This requires a deep capacity to trust oneself and others. It also slowly made me realise how trust was not only beneficial, but necessary for true human development and fulfilment. This truth was regardless of whether or not they could do themselves what they were asking others to do for them. I would even make a borderline conspiracy theory argument that the few (whether you call them the capitalist 1% or 'the powers that be') benefit from the many (us civilians) not manifesting the power of each other, as it would mean that it would be easier for them to maintain 'order'.

My perspective of trust was distorted. I subscribed to the school of thought that If I ever was going to get help that it should only be from people that would offer it and who were much better than me (in relation to what they were helping me with). The idea of proactively asking others for help was never something I would consider. On top of that, I didn't believe that people would even help me if I asked, so I was always ready to do things by myself. Even with that being said I would recall my severe discomfort with accepting help from others for the same reason that I wouldn't actively see it. In addition, I would see getting help as conceding to not being good enough. What would feel worse would be accepting help and feeling slowed down by that person's help (regardless of how good intentioned it was).

131

The foundational part of my belief system is me feeling that I had to become successful by myself for it to be valid. It also took me a while to realise the reason this was the case is because I didn't want to share the credit. But how did this take form? Going back to my childhood, I realised that I've felt casted in someone else's shadow for the majority of my life (Ironic how I can feel special and in someone's shadow at the same time). Can both feelings be valid?

Of course you can get to a point where you can do certain things without the present help of another human, but even then, there were people who would have helped you to get to that point. Therefore you didn't do it alone. Whilst going on the journey to identify why I was so obsessed with this self-made fallacy, I soon realised that I didn't actually want to achieve things alone...

I WANTED TO DO THINGS WITHOUT THE HELP OF THOSE WHO I HELD IN HIGH REGARD, SO I CAN SHOW THEM HOW SPECIAL I WAS AND GAIN THEIR APPROVAL

By that same extension, is my fear that they would disapprove one of the reasons why I struggle to ask people for help? Coming to think about it, approval has been the single biggest thing I've ever yearned for. It may be the same with all human beings but I can at the very least say that I yearn to win over the approval of others. However, what I yearned for even more than that was to not lose the approval of others. Having come across this truth, I strived to really start digging at the top and below the surface.

EXERCISE #30: APPROVAL LIST [WB PG 83]

Creating a list of those whose approval/disapproval affects me brought things even more into focus. My approval list was basically all the people that I either held in high regard during my childhood, or people I currently hold in high regard. I then realised that...

THE RELATIONSHIPS YOU HAVE WITH THE PEOPLE WHOSE APPROVAL YOU SEEK WILL PLAY A MASSIVE PART IN HOW YOU SEE RELATIONSHIPS, PERIOD.

The idea of winning someone's approval by asking them to help me with something was a ridiculous notion. If I asked someone whose approval I wanted to help me do something I felt would win over their approval, then automatically I wouldn't get their approval, right? This was the exact moment I realised something that I've mentioned previously in this book...

LIVING A LIFE OF TRYING TO GAIN OTHER PEOPLE'S APPROVAL IS UNHEALTHY

And I've realised that what played into my trust issues and my feeling that I need to do things alone is because my perspective on doing things with others was based on winning their approval. Not only that, but the process of trying to win someone over and not getting anything but copious approval, was simply tiring on the mind and the spirit. This perspective is simply not conducive to any form of success or happiness, never mind my own definition of it. I would have all of these goals and dreams and yet when it comes to interacting with the rest of the world, my frame of mind would be that I could only ever be loved if I won someone else's approval. What would be even more frustrating and increased my desire to do things alone, was experiencing the fact that people weren't as committed to winning my approval as I was to theirs (especially those I considered to be successful). I often felt like the people I observed to be successful were selfish, and I never wanted to be successful if it meant being that selfish. This was simply me not understanding true human nature and how the world truly works.

I finally made peace with the fact my definition of success, quite simply, is not something that I can achieve on my own. It's simply far too big a task to do (Lord knows I've tried). But at the same time I felt like I wasn't yet seeing the full picture. I had previously been doing things mainly 'by my-self' but yet I'd still been receiving help. So what is the next step in getting over my trust issues and manifesting the power of others?...

- 20 -
EXTERNAL PERSONAL BOUNDARIES (E.P.B)

"The only people who get upset about you setting boundaries are the ones who were benefiting from you having none"

Unknown

Another massive factor amongst many that have led to my trust issues is because I don't trust others to respect my boundaries. More importantly however is that **I've allowed** too many people to violate my boundaries on too many occasions. These include the boundaries that I didn't even explicitly communicate to others or even reconcile within myself.

NB: The moment where someone does something to you that truly bothers you personally, is the only sign you need that they have violated a boundary of yours.

What is important is truly understanding what bothers oneself. You may recall that I touched on internal personal boundaries earlier in the book and the reason why I mentioned it earlier and didn't immediately discuss external personal boundaries is because I feel it is important to gain real grounding in knowing and practising the protection of your personal rights against the worst part of yourself before you can then gain a grounding in protecting your personal rights against others and the rest of the world. You may also recall that I considered boundaries a true weakness of mine. Going deeper, I felt like having boundaries would be a sure fire way of soliciting unwanted disapproval from others. But this wasn't just a feeling. This was one of the things that I have felt more than comfortable depending on. This was one of the things I saw as my greatest ally...

THIS WAS AN ASSUMPTION

Assumption: A thing that is accepted as true or as certain to happen, <u>without proof</u>

Oxford Languages

Assumptions have felt like one of my strongest allies for the majority of life, but I didn't realise that these were assumptions because my previous life experience was all the painful proof I needed. But assumptions are more of an ally of fear than it has been to me personally. Assumptions have allowed me to feel protected from my own fears. Its' greatest benefit is being able to draw a conclusion without taking any real action. Doing this actually made me feel even smarter, almost as if I anticipated a potential threat and managed to avoid it, rather than attempting an action and experiencing what I feared. Growing up, one of my favourite TV shows was Hustle (the British version, not the American one). The tv show is about a team of con men and women, conning the unethical rich and trying to help the more ethical and in need along the way. Michael 'Mickey Bricks' Stone was the leader of the group and he was without a shadow of doubt one of my idols. What I loved about him was the fact that he pretty much always saw every possible scenario that could happen and was prepared for it (not to mention that he was also amazing at responding on the fly when something goes wrong that he didn't anticipate, even though he would bitterly hate doing so). I felt like it was a superhuman feat to anticipate all possible situations and make sure that the plan goes well regardless and I would try and model myself after him. I could use the excuse that I had the best of intentions when using assumptions, as it is used in maths and science when it comes to creating theories. I felt better for them. But I have to ask myself the question ....

"WHAT IF YOU'VE CONFUSED ASSUMPTIONS WITH INTELLIGENCE?"

And the reality is I have. Assumptions are a part of intelligence but they aren't the whole story. The reason why is because if I were to follow the same example of science and maths, there would be assumptions (and more specifically there would be hypotheses in science) but one thing I forgot was **those assumptions and hypotheses will be tested** before a conclusion is drawn. It's true my previous experiences may have value, but maybe their value is in me drawing (and being prepared to test) a hypothesis rather than trying to draw an assumptive conclusion from previous experience alone.

Earlier in the book (more specifically in Reason 2) I touched on internal expectations, assumptions and the concept of Internal Sense of Should. I feel that assumptions fall more into the external realm of life and I realised that my assumptions of others were negative, which definitely was an ally in strengthening my trust issues with others. This also has two sides to it, my assumptions of how people _will_ be around me, and my expectations of how I feel they _should_ be around me.. I wanted to explore this further...

EXERCISE #31: EXTERNAL SENSE OF SHOULD QUESTIONNAIRE [WB PG 84]

I expected people to treat me as the special person that I always saw myself, but at the same time I assumed that they wouldn't bother. This level of cognitive dissonance simply isn't healthy or sustainable in the long term. The gap between how I expected others to see me and treat me was the polar opposite to my assumptions of the same thing. Upon realising this, it made sense why I would feel such immense levels of frustration at the idea of trusting others. It also dawned on me that people who matched my external sense of should were phenomenal about something that I had always struggled with ... boundaries, for both themselves and for others to live by.

It's ironic, as boundaries actually help to build trust, yet I felt scared to use boundaries because I thought it signified that there was no trust. To deepen the irony, I didn't trust people anyway (I just didn't want them to know about it). That was my mistake because even though harmony is important, one should never personally suffer, just to make someone else happy or comfortable. My philosophy of boundaries was to respect everyone else's and **assume** that people would respect mine, even though I wouldn't tell them what they were. Whenever a boundary of mine would get violated, I'd be more offended because in my mind my boundaries were not only obvious, but they were more than reasonable, as well as the fact that people should already know not to cross them. How wrong I truly was. And that's where External Personal Boundaries come in.

So how do I know if I have an External Personal Boundary? Whilst there are similarities with the internal personal boundaries mentioned earlier in the book, here is a checklist I put together that you can follow.

- ☐ You have identified The Boundary
- ☐ You've established the clear right(s) the boundary is designed to protect
- ☐ You have determined a consequence(s) to anyone who violates that boundary
- ☐ You've identified and pre-established exception(s) to the boundary
- ☐ You have communicated the boundary to yourself (in writing or via self talk)
- ☐ You have communicated it to others (Verbally or non verbally)
- ☐ You have determined a consequence(s) for yourself if you fail to enforce the boundary
- ☐ You have enforced a boundary that someone has violated.

Example: Jane & not wanting people to come and visit her at her home unannounced

1. No one can come to visit without calling first (24hrs in advance minimum)
2. Jane's right to her own personal time and space
3. Jane won't answer the door if someone violates this boundary.
4. Jane informed those who visit her that the only exception to her boundary is if it's an emergency.
5. Jane has verbally said this to and texted her friends, family and anyone else who would normally visit.
6. Jane set a consequence that for any occasion she didn't enforce this boundary (where there were no valid exceptions present) she wouldn't eat her favourite ice cream that evening.
7. Michelle (Jane's friend) came to visit unannounced and Jane didn't answer the door. Michelle then called Jane, in which Jane clearly stated that Michelle didn't call ahead and thus wouldn't be allowed in as she has made other plans.

Internal and External boundaries go together, but the reason why external boundaries weren't discussed earlier is because enforcing your boundaries on others can only be so strong if you haven't learnt to enforce boundaries upon yourself. I figured this out as I was trying to enforce boundaries. I struggled massively, and I strongly feel that it was more of a challenge that I was asking others to do for me what I wasn't prepared to do for myself. Boundaries and how you navigate them is also a great way of assessing how you treat yourself. To treat yourself well would be to be aware of each and every violation of your boundary and enforce the consequences immediately. The quicker you do this, the more you are showing your mind, body and spirit that YOU CARE and that YOU MATTER. Love begins with self love, and boundaries and the protection of your rights is right up there with the strongest forms of self love.

So you may be asking the question, "What do I do if someone around me keeps ignoring and/or violating my boundaries?" The answer is simple…

MINIMISE AND/OR CUT OFF THE PEOPLE FROM YOUR LIFE WHO DON'T RESPECT YOUR BOUNDARIES

The reason I said minimise as well as cut off is because cutting off some people may not yet be possible. An example of this is someone that you live with or depend on to put a roof over your head (e.g. parents/guardians). The true end goal should always be to cut off any and everyone who doesn't respect your boundaries (after attempts on your side to solicit respect), but you may need to start with minimising. The biggest thing that others need to understand is that you have boundaries, they can't violate those boundaries without consequences and that if you enforce a consequence, it is down to their own choices/decisions. Through minimising alone, you may find that people start treating you differently and become more respectful of your boundaries. In those cases the choice is up to you how much you want to interact with them in your life

But anyway, enough of the talking, let's get to work…

EXERCISE #32: E.P.B CHART [WB PG 87]

Trying to work on trust issues without establishing your boundaries is always going to present problems, simply because another boundary of yours being violated by someone else would be all that it would take to undermine any progress you would have made. Part of this problem with boundaries goes back to Reason 1 (not feeling good enough). If you are feeling stuck at this stage and haven't read Reason 1, I'd strongly recommend doing so, before coming back to this section. Boundaries aren't just an event, they are part of a lifestyle choice. Yes you may end up losing relationships because of this. If that were the case, that is just God/The Universe showing you that they were unhealthy relationships. You'll soon release after the initial fear and dread, that you feel a lot more in control and a lot happier as a result.

Now I've gone through the process of letting go and setting up boundaries, it's time to truly get into manifesting the power of people

21

MANIFESTING THE POWER OF PEOPLE

"The power of the people is much stronger than the people in power"
Wael Ghonim

People are complex and this isn't about breaking down all elements of all people. Doing this would be far too time consuming (and also something that I'm not qualified for). Additionally, doing so wouldn't really serve as an added benefit in the journey to happiness and success. This is more about understanding enough about people to manifest their power. So you may be wondering 'How can I utilise the power of people?'. Here is my blueprint that I discovered on this journey, which we will walk through in this chapter

Identify your definition of success

Identify the people who can increase your chances of achieving your definition of success, as well as how they can help.

Find them and Identify *their* definition of success(s) and how you can help with that.

Build mutually beneficial relationships: Ask those people for help and strive to help them with their best interests.

Evaluate their help, if they made a mistake or betrayed your trust, forgive them and look for learning lessons. If they done well, express gratitude and also look for learning lessons (be thankful regardless)

Go Back to Step 1

Reason 0 covered the first step. If you have already read that section and done the work, the other steps should be much easier (if you haven't, I'd recommend you do). What hasn't been covered are the other three steps. The second step is massively important. Have you ever been offered help by someone or many people along the lines of 'if you need anything, let me know how I can help'? But at the same time you didn't take them up on it because you didn't quite know/believe how they could actually help? This has been most of my life. But true interdependence is about teams and team work

To truly manifest the power of people, I understood that it is important to develop a better understanding of what trust truly is, how it works and how it can be used to improve the chances of achieving happiness/ success.

THE QUESTION WE SHOULD BE ASKING OURSELVES ISN'T WHETHER OR NOT A PERSON CAN BE TRUSTED, IT SHOULD BE...WHAT CAN I TRUST THEM WITH?

I definitely saw trust as a yes or no question. Can I trust you or not? If I trusted you, I trusted you with anything and everything. Just becoming aware of my truth when it came to this further explains my history of trust issues. As the late rapper Earl 'DMX' Simmons said…

"Trust everyone to be themselves, but trust that you see them well"

My conclusion, after much reflection, is that at our worst...

HUMANS WILL MAKE DECISIONS BASED ON WHAT THEY FEEL IS ULTIMATELY IN THEIR BEST INTEREST

And at our best...

HUMANS WILL MAKE DECISIONS BASED ON THEIR SENSE OF RIGHT AND WRONG

This is important to understand because it makes it easier to understand what we should trust different people with and to what extent. It doesn't matter how trustworthy an accountant is, you couldn't trust them to fix your plumbing. That doesn't mean they aren't to be trusted in general, just in that particular context.

What I realised was important was that before I could come up with a list of people that could help me, it was important to genuinely understand the concept of other people period. I broke this down into what I call the 12 pillars of people. These 12 pillars apply to two categories: You and Other People. It is important to make this distinction because manifesting the power of power is about navigating through these 12 pillars and creating a mutually beneficial exchange between the two categories. You may end up getting an overwhelming amount of other people's pillars and a lot of them won't even necessarily want the same in return. The only thing that the universe would ask for is for you to put the same amount into others who may not be able to give but truly need to receive. That's the general concept of charity. You may give your money to other people who can't give you money back but their gratitude and how they make use of that money will spiritually pay you back more than money ever could.

For the sake of simplicity I will also abbreviate the two types of people to M (My) and OP (Other People's). The 12 pillars are the following

1. Dreams - MD | OPD
2. Needs & Wants - MNW | OPNW
3. Time - MT | OPT
4. Energy - ME | OPE
5. Relationships/Network - MR | OPR
6. Money - MM | OPM
7. Labour - ML | OPL
8. Resources - MRes | OPRes
9. Systems - MS | OPS
10. Knowledge - MK | OPK
11. Experiences - MEx | OPEx
12. Ideas - MI | OPI

DREAMS - MD | OPD

Dreams are very much the items that you would have on your bucket list of things that you would love to do before you reach the end of your life. This forms the definition of happiness/success mentioned in Reason 0. Other people however may have completely different dreams to you and that's what makes life truly beautiful. Another element of this beauty is that other people's dreams can complement your own and each other's. The synergy between dreams is something that can dramatically improve the health and quality of relationships. You should minimise the relationships you have with people whose dreams clash with yours. It's very easy to prioritise other people's dreams over your own and not too many other people may be invested in your dreams.

<u>Guide Questions</u>

<u>MD</u>

Do I know my dreams?

Do I pursue my dreams?

How can I pursue my dreams?

Do other people help me with my dreams?

How can other people help me with my dreams?

<u>OPD</u>

Do other people know their own dreams?

Do other people pursue their dreams?

How can other people pursue their dreams?

Do I help other people with their dreams?

How can I help other people discover/pursue their dreams?

NEEDS & WANTS - MNW | OPNW

This concept is pretty straightforward, however it's important to recognise that people's needs and wants can also vastly differ from your own. Needs and wants are typically more short term (in comparison to dreams) but can also vary depending on the circumstances and situation. Personal rights and boundaries will fall within this category also.

<u>Guide Questions</u>

<u>MNW</u>

What are my needs and wants?

Do I cater to my needs and wants?

Do other people cater to my needs and wants?

Do other people help me cater to my own needs and wants?

How can other people cater to my needs and wants?

OPNW

What are other people's needs and wants?

Do other people cater to their own needs and wants?

Do I cater to other people's needs and wants?

How can I cater to other people's needs and wants?

Do I help other people cater to their own needs and wants?

How can I help other people cater to their own needs and wants?

TIME - MT | OPT

One of the most valued pillars of a person. Time is literally the only pillar that can be given and yet can't be taken back.

Guide Questions

MT

How much of my time do I give to myself?

How much of their time do other people give to me?

How much of my time do I give to other people?

How can I receive other people's time?

How can I best use my time?

How can other people's time save me time?

OPT

How much of their own time do other people give to themselves?

How can other people best use their time?

How can my time help other people best use their time?

How can I help other people save time?

ENERGY - ME | OPE

This is what can greatly affect the quality of one's time. I'd argue that this is the most important pillar of a person (along with time). This translates to not just physical energy, but mental, emotional and spiritual energy.

Guide Questions

ME

How are my current energy levels?

How much of my energy do I invest in myself?

How much of their energy do other people invest in me?

How can I increase my energy levels?

What are my signs of fatigue?

OPE

What are other people's energy levels

How much of their own energy do other people invest in themselves?

How much of my energy do I invest in other people?

RELATIONSHIPS/NETWORK - MR | OPR

This pillar is concerning the network of relationships that a person has; both personally and professionally.

Guide Questions

MR

Do my relationships/network increase or decrease my chances of achieving my definition of success?

What new relationship(s) do I need to establish?

What current relationships do I need to cultivate?

Which relationships no longer serve me?

OPR

Do my relationships increase or decrease the chances of other people achieving their definition of success

Who would benefit from having a relationship with me?

How can I help other people with their relationships?

148

MONEY - MM | OPM

They say this makes the world go round. This has also become a difficult topic for many people (often due to the fact that they haven't learned how to master this part of their lives)

<u>Guide Questions</u>

<u>MM</u>

How much money do I make? & is it enough?

How can I make more money?

How much money do I spend? And is it sustainable?

What better ways could I be using my money?

How much of other people's money do I receive?

How can other people increase the amount of money I have?

How can I use other people's money to achieve my definition of success

<u>OPM</u>

What are the spending habits of other people around me? & is it sustainable?

What can other people do to increase the amount of money they have

How can I help other people with their income?

How can I help other people with their spending habits?

How can other people use my money to achieve their definition of happiness?

LABOUR - ML | OPL

This includes your work and any creations (e.g. work as an employee at a company or having an employee work in your company). This is often calculated on a time basis, but can also be calculated by the end product.

ML

How much of my labour do I give to myself?

How much of my labour do I give to others?

How can I best use my labour?

OPL

How much of other people's labour do I utilise?

How much other people's labour do they give to other people?

How can I best ask for and use other people's labour?

RESOURCES - MRES | OPRES

This concerns things that one owns, controls and/or has access to (e.g. rental property, office space, etc)

MRes

How well do I utilise my resources for myself?

How much of my resources do I extend to others?

OPRes

How do other people utilise their resources?

How much of other people's resources are offered to me?

How much of other people's resources do I utilise?

SYSTEMS - MS | OPS

These are methods as to how to do something (e.g. Buying a McDonald's franchise, where you would be using their business systems). This synergies with knowledge, the difference is systems are knowledge applied into practical steps that are also tried and tested.

Guide Questions

MS

Do I have systems? And if so, how effective are they in helping me?

How many of my systems have I shared with others?

How much can other people contribute to my own systems?

OPS

How have other people's systems added to other people's lives?

How much of other people's systems do I use?

How can other people's systems add to my life?

KNOWLEDGE - MK | OPK

This pillar has become so much easier to access. With the power of the internet and platforms like YouTube, more and more knowledge is widely available. A distinction needs to be made between information and knowledge however. There is a wide amount of information but information may not always be accurate (due to the fact that with the internet, anyone can publish information). Knowledge however is information that has been applied and proved true for a significant number of people.

Guide Questions

MK

How does my knowledge add to my life?

How can I use my knowledge to add to my life?

How much of my knowledge do I share with other people?

OPK

How much of other people's knowledge can I access?

How much of other people's knowledge do I seek?

How much do I utilise other people's knowledge?

How can other people's knowledge add to my life?

EXPERIENCES - MEX | OPEX

This pillar is one of the greatest sources for knowledge and ideas (as well as other pillars). Shared experiences are also one of the greatest ways of establishing and deepening connections with other people.

Guide Questions

MEx

How can I use my experiences to add value to my life?

Which of my experiences can I share with other people?

How can other people learn from my experiences?

OPEx

How can I learn from other people's experiences?

How can other people's experiences add value to my life?

IDEAS - MI | OPI

This one is often put on a pedestal and as a consequence, its importance is overvalued (All you need to do is study enough business stories to know). What you do with the idea is far more important than the idea itself. Ideas can be the spark to the manifestation of many of the other pillars.

Guide Questions

MI

How much of my ideas do I make use of?

How much do my ideas increase my chances of success & happiness?

How much of my ideas do I give to other people?

What value can my ideas add to other people?

OPI

How many ideas do other people offer me?

What value can other people's ideas add to me?

How can I utilise other people's ideas?

You may have noticed a lot of guide questions, which can be a lot to take in. These are an extension of the following six core questions you should ask yourself and to get to the heart of manifesting the power of people is to ask yourself these questions? Another point to mention is that you don't necessarily need every pillar of people, the questions are designed to help you assess which one(s) you do need and give you a good standing to improve the way in which you utilise them (or to even start utilising them)...

1. How much of my pillars do I give to myself?
2. How much of my pillars do I give to others?
3. How much of the pillars do others give to me?
4. How much of the pillars do others give to themselves?
5. How can other people's pillars add value to my life?
6. How can my pillars add value to other people's lives?

VALUE #7 KNOW YOUR LIMITATIONS

When I went through these questions it made me realise that I had been relying far too much on solely my own pillars for my life and have given far too much of my pillars to others, whilst not being open to receiving from other people. This made me look again into my realisation that I love helping others but I saw the idea of accepting help as a sign of weakness and proof of limitation. The thing is however, we all have limitations. Additionally, our limitations have a purpose of bringing us closer together. Looking at the pillars, I eventually realised that I don't even have enough to provide for myself, never mind others, and I wasn't supposed to. Before doing this work I saw help as a short term exchange until I can do it myself but this value helped me realise that one's limitations are a good thing that brings oneself closer to others, rather than a bad thing that needs to quickly be eradicated.

My final realisation was the most profound ...

THERE ARE OTHER PEOPLE WHO ARE MORE THAN HAPPY TO GIVE THEIR PILLARS TO OTHERS, AND YOU

This is also in part to the fact that truly mature people recognise that they also have limitations. I made the assumption that other people wouldn't be happy to give their pillars to me if I just asked and you either gave or you received. I was wrong. Manifesting the power of people is to give AND receive. Some people only give, some people only receive, but true harmony is when you do both. I gave far more than I ever received and as a result I felt bitter. I'd be giving people my pillars that I didn't feel I could ever ask to receive. This realisation as to how this has been holding me back from achieving my definition of success made it even easier to change. Not trusting other people's pillars and being sceptical of their intentions behind offering it went against human nature. From working on reason 1 I realised that i didn't believe that I deserved to ask for help because I didn't feel I deserved to receive it.

The starting point for the pillars are dreams, needs and wants. This is simply because these pillars will often dictate how we utilise our other pillars (if we do at all). Before getting into how dreams, needs and wants of others can help, it's important to start thinking about what other people's dreams, needs and wants are. The best way to do that? With people that you already care about...

EXERCISE #33: OP-DNW CHART [WB PG 88]

Doing this exposed the fact that I didn't know as much about the people i cared about as I had thought. Many of the people that I cared about were people whose dreams I felt I knew but not to a strong enough extent. I had also realised that I had assumed a lot of their needs and wants. I then took it upon myself to ask people what their dreams, needs and wants were. I was truly surprised about the things that had come up. What was more of a surprise was quite simply how much more there was to their dreams.

The next step consisted of me asking myself, "How can I apply the 12 pillars of people to add value to my life?" The short answer is …

USE YOUR PILLARS AND THE OTHER PEOPLE'S PILLARS TO HELP YOU ACHIEVE YOURS (AS WELL AS OTHERS') DEFINITION OF SUCCESS

This process can start simply by starting with a simple goal and identifying which pillars would be useful to help achieve that goal, in addition to identifying how each useful pillar can actually help you achieve the goal. Using your own pillars is easier to understand, but in the context of manifesting the power of people, other people's pillars will be the focus….

EXERCISE #34: OP QUESTIONNAIRE [WB PG 90]

Doing this helped me immensely. It opened me up to how much I can improve as a person, just by allowing others into my life. It also made me realise how much I've truly developed as a person from other people and the pillars they have given to me. Without realising, the power of people has blessed me beyond my wildest dreams. It seems funny now that I previously resisted the idea of doubling down on something that has done so much for me. I would say that this was due to me focusing on only the negative times in which I had been affected by other people and their pillars. With that being said, this book isn't about being one long therapy session.

It's about digging into one self long enough to get to the practical stuff and produce tangible results. With that being said the next step is to really add other people to my goals and definition of success...

EXERCISE #35: HELP LIST [WB PG 91]

In my case, the people who could help me were already in my vicinity and they were already helping me or were just waiting to be asked. I can be sensitive to the fact that this may not be the case for other people but if you did do this exercise you may realise that there is more help around you than you thought.

With that being said, what if you don't know where to start? Here's a non exhaustive chart to help you (Note: as technology can change over time, I'll stick to categories rather than specifics)

PILLAR	SOURCES OF HELP
Dreams	Success Stories (e.g. video on Youtube), Motivational content, Self Reflection, Spiritual Mentors, Therapists, Counsellors, Life Coaches
Needs & Wants	Self Reflection, Spiritual Mentors, Therapists, Counsellors, Life Coaches
Time	Personal relationship network (friends/family/etc), Communities. Time saving technology (e.g. a microwave)
Energy	Personal and professional relationship network (friends/family/etc), Communities, Nutritionist (Diet), Personal Trainer (Fitness)

Relation-ships/Network	Communities, Social Connectors, Relationship Coaches
Money	Job/Career, Business Income, Savings, Banks (Loans & Grants), Peer to Peer Lending
Labour	Employment Agencies (Offline or Online)
Resources	Online Search Engines (E.g. Google), Online Video Platforms (e.g. YouTube), Social Media Platforms (e.g. Instagram), Books, Mentors
Systems	Online Search Engines (E.g. Google), Online Video Platforms (e.g. YouTube), Social Media Platforms (e.g. Instagram), Books, Mentors
Knowledge	Online Search Engines (E.g. Google), Online Video Platforms (e.g. YouTube), Social Media Platforms (e.g. Instagram), Books, Mentors
Experiences	Online Search Engines (E.g. Google), Online Video Platforms (e.g. YouTube), Social Media Platforms (e.g. Instagram), Books, Mentors, Friends
Ideas	Online Search Engines (E.g. Google), Online Video Platforms (e.g. YouTube), Social Media Platforms (e.g. Instagram), Books, Mentors, personal network (e.g. friends/family/etc)

Once I had a good understanding of the different sources for each pillar, it was then important to regularly ask for help and keep a record of what happened. My previous mindset was that asking for help was more hassle than it was worth. Furthermore, it rarely helped. It now makes sense why I wouldn't bother trying to manifest the power of people if my recollection of the experience was negative...

EXERCISE #36: HELP JOURNAL [WB PG 92]

This was where I experienced my most profound breakthrough during this journey to address this reason that I wasn't successful…. Yet. It made me realise…

OTHER PEOPLE DON'T NEED TO HAVE HELPED YOU 100% TO HOW YOU WANTED THEM TO, FOR THEM TO HAVE ACTUALLY HELPED YOU

This black or white mindset I previously had robbed me of the added value of even receiving help that was to 30% of my standards/liking. The most beautiful thing about other people isn't just about the pillars that they can offer, it's that regardless of how much or how little they help, they almost always provide opportunities for you to learn and grow. From who to ask for help, to feedback on how you can better help others. On top of that, whatever goes wrong always makes for a great story to tell someone. The knowledge I have received from other people in life and in this journey from writing this book came from those other people sharing a story with me on their failures, which supported the knowledge they were blessing me with.

> *"Only a fool learns from his own mistakes.*
> *The wise man learns from the mistakes of others"*
> Otto Von Bismarck

Just what if your mistakes were designed to help yourself AND others? Additionally, what if other people's mistakes were designed to help you save your time and energy? (a true example of another person's pillar helping your own). Manifesting the power of people would have been much more difficult for me if I didn't work on the other reasons why I wasn't successful… yet. How could I ask for help if I didn't know what my definition of success was? It would have ended up with the blind leading the blind. How could I ask for and receive help if I didn't believe that I was good enough to deserve it? Even if it was offered, I would have poorly utilised it, and maybe even thrown it back in peoples' faces. How could I ask for and receive help if I didn't feel like I could handle life and the things that come with it? The help would have just fallen on death ears.

Earlier in the book, I touched on my value of treating myself the way I want to be treated. I'm aware that this value at its extreme can lead to selfishness, when it is designed to develop one's self interest. The difference between self interest and selfishness is the fact that selfishness is acknowledging that your needs are mostly more important (to you) than someone else's'. Selfishness on the other hand is believing that ONLY your needs matter. I say that because filling your own cup is the best way you are able to consistently fill the cups of other people around you. I have long neglected myself and often put others ahead of me. How could I then expect people to treat me better than I treat myself?. I learned that how you treat yourself is spiritual communication to others as to how you want to be treated. This goes back to your External Sense of Should. Use the way you wish to be seen as the basis to treat yourself, so that others can follow suit and treat you the same way.

GROUND THREE - HABITUALS

1. **Hurt List** - Review your hurt list once a week
2. **Forgiveness Letter** - Write a forgiveness letter to one person a eek
3. **Villain List** - Review on a monthly basis
4. **Approval List** - Review on a monthly basis
5. **E.P.B Chart** - Review on a weekly basis

REASON FOUR:

I FEEL IT REQUIRES MORE WORK/SACRIFICE THAN IT'S WORTH

SIGNS & SYMPTOMS THAT YOU ARE SUFFERING FROM THIS INCLUDE, BUT ARE NOT LIMITED TO;

1. Procrastination
2. Unrealised Potential
3. Looking for and/or getting involved in get-rich-quick schemes
4. Seeking opportunities with 'guarantees'
5. Risk-Aversion

OBJECTIVE(S):

1. To identify the work and sacrifice(s) necessary to achieve one's definition of success
2. To confirm one's definition of success that justifies the work and sacrifice required

My Truth

I don't mind working hard. The issue I have though is when I feel that I have to work harder than I'm comfortable with, I need to feel that not only will the end result justify the work I'm putting in, but the positive end result is 'guaranteed'. If I don't feel any of these two things, then I often procrastinate and/or stop altogether.

The harder I work, the greater the sense of expectancy and entitlement I feel towards whatever it is I'm working on. My biggest fear is working hard on something, going beyond my comfort zone to accomplish it; to then fail. Even worse would be to succeed and feel that the end result wasn't worth the amount of effort I put into it. It has happened to me before and when it has happened, it has left me feeling hollow.

If I feel that the end result is guaranteed. I will work the long hours, make the sacrifices and the 'blood, sweat and tears' necessary will be seen as a fair trade. If however I have the smallest amount of doubt about succeeding, it's likely my mind will protect me from walking the first step, in anticipation that I can put all that effort in further down the line to no avail. I often would base my decisions on the following list of questions:

1. *Do I have to do it?*
2. *Is the effort I have to put into this going to be more than I'm comfortable with?*
3. *Is the outcome worth more than the level of discomfort/sacrifice required of me.*
4. *If so, is the outcome guaranteed?*

Imagine you are in a car and in front of you are 10 traffic lights, 10 metres apart from each other. I'm the person that won't feel comfortable driving until all 10 traffic lights turn green at the same time. I've only felt comfortable if the whole path was clear, and if there were any significant hurdles, I would make the conclusion that the path simply wasn't worth going down.

22

WHAT'S YOUR LIFE LIKE?

"Everyone wants to go to heaven, but no one wants to die"

Albert King

How often do you ask yourself that question? And to what degree? Before even starting this section, it's important for me to explain how much asking myself that question and putting it in writing has truly helped with my mood and with my true sense of where I am. It's so easy to think your life isn't going great without too much evidence. But keeping track of things truly can help you regain perspective on where you are. In similar fashion to Reason 0, this section may help you (as it has helped me) feel better about where you are going or at the very least develop a clear idea of where you are going wrong. To keep things simple on this journey, I simply identified the categories that matter to me in life and I made a point on a weekly to mark out of 10 how I felt about my progress in each one. I previously was marking myself based on how I felt about my results, but I realised that there is more value to progress than results. I hope these next few chapters share insight to you as to why that is the case.

EXERCISE #37: WEEKLY LIFE ASSESSMENT [WB PG 96]

Doing this actually helped me realise that I was spending so much of my time pursuing wealth (in terms of hours during the week) and was neglecting the other parts of my life that I considered important. Not only that, I didn't even feel good about my progress, or lack thereof, in pursuing wealth. It's interesting how many of us want what we want, because we feel that it will change our lives. Without a shadow of a doubt, if I achieved even a fraction of my definition of success it would change my life forever. The biggest irony of all however is I realised that you have to change your life FIRST before you can achieve your definition of success. This realisation came from me studying countless people who I would consider successful or excellent at what they do. I had been studying them from the lens of 'What do they do?', 'What do I need to do to also be successful'. This led to trying to find tips and tricks from those who were successful so that I can be the same. This led to me seeing an overwhelming amount of work that would need to be done. This to me felt daunting and as a result I would just about be prepared to do it if the result was guaranteed. What I truly didn't realise then, but do now, is the fact that...

SUCCESS IS DETERMINED BY HOW YOU <u>LIVE</u>, NOT WHAT YOU <u>DO</u>

Everyone that I had studied, ABSOLUTELY EVERYONE, had done this. I never wanted to dedicate my life to my career (at the time this was music), simply because I felt that it wouldn't be conducive to the other goals that were important to me (e.g. having a family). But it's not necessarily your life you need to dedicate to something, it's **your lifestyle.** What is the difference between your life and your lifestyle? Your life is literally the eternity of your life, from when you decide you want to dedicate your life to something, to the very day that you die. I was under the false impression that to truly be successful or excellent in music would require dedicating my life. This was something I pushed back against (mentally at least) and was probably the reason why I pursued music with not as much tenacity as I should have. I had seen countless people I had studied (some of which I personally knew) sacrifice what I saw as pieces of their humanity for their success. I simply felt like this wasn't a fair trade and tried pursuing music without making their type of sacrifices. One thing about me which I've mentioned in this book is the fact that because I was told early in life that I'm gifted, I carried the belief that I could bypass the rules that the rest of the 'average' people have to abide by. You can dedicate your life to something, but it doesn't mean you have the right lifestyle. Lifestyle on the other hand is very much about what you do on a daily, weekly, monthly, and so on basis. Many of us when we watch who are successful, we may see that the biggest things that seem to be pushed forward to our vicinity is the success part, the interviews, the flashy material things (cars, houses), the super polished suits & dresses, the lights, glitz & glamour. What we don't see often enough however, is the hard work, the countless hours of doing things that the average person wouldn't be comfortable doing (waking up anytime before 6am in the morning everyday is a great example)

I often felt like If I wasn't achieving what I wanted to, then it meant that I had to change everything. What I didn't realise was the sheer fact that I may have just needed to make tweaks. Experience has taught me that real and sustainable changes are a collection of smaller changes. Before I tried changing anything, I needed to run a full diagnosis on my current lifestyle. This was only part 1 of what I see as a 3 step process...

1. Assess your current lifestyle
2. Study the lifestyle(s) of those who you consider to be successful and identify commonalities
3. Align your current lifestyle with the commonalities of the lifestyle(s) of those you consider successful

The biggest part of doing this saw me trying to change my lifestyle on the spot the second I became more aware of it. But as a nutritionist would require you to do a food journal across a period of time, they would often require you to journal **based on what you currently eat, rather than trying to change it during the journal**. The reason this is needed is because this is the diagnostics stage, where the more accurate the reading, the more effective the plan going forward will be. In similar fashion, if a food inspector comes to inspect a restaurant when the restaurant knows about it, they are more likely to clean and improve their hygiene habits just for the sake of passing the inspection, where a more accurate reading would be an inspection that the restaurant didn't know about. But let me see what my life is like this time around, with zero judgement on it. The zero judgement part is even more important because without out, it will be difficult to develop an accurate picture on one's accurate situation.

EXERCISE #38: CURRENT LIFESTYLE MAP [WB PG 99]

rom doing this I became a lot more aware and present with the habitual choices I would be making. It was actually difficult to not want to change my habits there and then. Not only that, I realised how much of a challenge I have had with maintaining discipline (a skill that is vital in any form of success). I've always struggled with self discipline and I've often felt that my 'specialness' can be the reason why I achieve things in quantum leaps rather than small, consistent and daily action. The idea of small daily actions or 'doing the basics' felt boring to me. As I've mentioned earlier in the book, I got a kick out of showing off and showing people how special I was. With that being said there is much more work to be done to truly assess my current lifestyle. I asked myself the question...

WHAT WOULD YOUR LIFE LOOK LIKE IN THE FUTURE IF YOU CONTINUED LIVING THE EXACT SAME WAY AS YOU DO NOW?

EXERCISE #39: FUTURE LIFE FORECAST [WB PG 101]

In doing this It dawned on me how far out of alignment my lifestyle was to the life I wanted to have and the person I truly wanted to be. It was humbling and truly put things in perspective for me. Lifestyle is also a reflection of one's life philosophy (even if it wasn't by conscious design). I then made a resolution to examine all of the necessary elements of my life and lifestyle so that I can truly address this issue...

- 23 -
WHAT IS YOUR DIET?

"Your diet isn't only what you eat. It's what you watch, It's what you read, it's what you listen to, so I'm mindful of what i ingest"

Saul Williams

"You can't out-train a bad diet"

Unknown

Before starting this journey I had only seen my diet as meaning what I ate and drank. I soon realised that not only was it much more than that, but it would play such a factor in me achieving success. In that case, what is your diet? In no order, I feel that they are:

1. What you eat & drink
2. What you watch (E.G. TV/Films)
3. What you read (e.g. Books/Newspapers/Magazines)
4. What you listen to (e.g. Music/Podcasts/Audio Books)
5. Who you talk to and spend time with (e.g. Family/Friends/ Significant Other)
6. What community(s) are you a part of (e.g. Social groups, Organisations)

WHAT YOU EAT & DRINK

Growing up and throughout my adulthood I mainly drink water, but what I eat has been completely out of whack from the health goals that I've always wanted for myself. I wanted to be the guy with the six pack and the herculean physique. I didn't want to go as far as the bodybuilder type but I wanted to be lean and be ridiculously stronger than I might look. I've been in and out of the gym for years (almost decades at this point) in this pursuit but I've always been impatient and fell short. The idea of working out I enjoyed, but it only felt worth continuing if I got the results I was looking for immediately. I had been told that diet was also important in this endeavour but I was too attached to the food I loved to eat, whilst also thinking that I could get away with working the way I wanted to. As I studied more and more about physique, I discovered, but chose to run away from the fact that your diet is actually the biggest factor in your physique (outside of genetics).

I also had a juvenile impression of dieting. My impression of diet was that it was for those who were obese and needed to lose weight. Not only that, I saw diet as a temporary fix where you basically give up everything you like to eat, to eat things that you hate. The only catch being that you would only need to suffer for a short period of time and never would have to go through the ordeal again. I'm very aware of how I'm phrasing this, because I truly saw it as this extreme. To add more elements to this impression, I didn't even want to lose weight, I just wanted muscles. I would consider myself skinny fat, where I didn't have the muscles that I wanted, and yet I always had a pot belly. At first I struggled to understand why. I thought I would either be skinny or overweight. Another factor that isn't appreciated enough is how diet can affect one's state of mind…

EXERCISE #40: CURRENT DIET [WB PG 102]

From doing this I was staggered by how much my current and previous diets were accurate reflections of where I was at that relevant time of my life. This also made me realise how I had seen change as a short term method of getting what I want, in the sense of changing my behaviour and either going back to old behaviours if I had achieved what I wanted, or if what I

169

wanted didn't happen fast enough. This also overwhelmed me to no end to realise my diet can affect my chances of success. The thing that did give me much comfort was the fact that all of these things were actually things that I had the power to control.

HOW MUCH OF MY TIME DO I ACTUALLY SPEND ON ACHIEVING MY DEFINITION OF SUCCESS?

The simple answer to this question was simply not enough. That being said, discovering this led me to wanting to change things in quantum leaps, but that simply isn't' the answer. Sustainable change happens bit by bit and can go faster simply by allowing momentum to snowball one's efforts. I have tried on many occasions to do the opposite but it ended in frustration. As they say, for you to get a different result, you need to be prepared to become different. Identifying your current food and drink diet is the primer for the next step in the journey, identifying one's other diets (which I will call one's terrain)...

THE TERRAIN 102: WHAT IS 'YOUR TERRAIN'

"Sheep are always looking for a new shepherd when the terrain gets rocky"
Karen Marie Moning

Accepting the fact that was a terrain that affected me was challenging enough, but what I found even more challenging was identifying all of its elements. Due to my inflated ego, I always felt like the terrain wasn't important, as I was gifted enough to get to where I wanted to regardless of how good or bad the terrain could be. In my mind, everything in life should and would go my way *as long as I really wanted the outcome*. On reflection, this was a childish perspective, but I wouldn't be the first or the last to share this school of thought. Where I would see the terrain as non-existent, many others may see the terrain as an inescapable prison. I have observed so many people in life who see themselves as victims of their own circumstances or feel permanently held back by people around them (See 'The Victim vs The Hero...' Chapter, if you haven't already). Even more alarming are those who feel their terrain is doing them a favour by holding them back. It's hard to navigate the terrain if you feel like it's protecting you.

THE FIRST STEP TO DEALING WITH
ANYTHING IS TO ACCEPT THAT IT EXISTS

I elaborated on this when I first brought up the Terrain in Reason 0. Many of my issues got bigger and bigger, primarily due to the fact that I refused to acknowledge that it existed and (even more dangerously) I refused to acknowledge that it impacted me. The idea that anything or anyone could hold me back went against my self image that I could do anything, and that conflict I feel held me back even further. To accept your terrain isn't to accept that things will never change, it's to accept the challenges you will probably need to go through. Some of you reading this may think of obstacles when thinking of your journey to success but I feel what helped me was seeing obstacles as challenges. Furthermore I had to ask myself…

WHAT IF, WHAT YOU SAW AS OBSTACLES, WAS ACTUALLY DESIGNED TO BE TRAINING FOR YOU TO BECOME THE PERSON YOU WAS TRULY MEANT TO BE?

If this were the case, it would be a lot easier to accept, that's for sure. Identifying and accepting your terrain is also humbling and may provide perspective on why you may not be successful… yet. As I kept trying and failing with addressing this issue, it felt like I discovered a part of the truth, rather than the whole truth.

THE TERRAIN IN ITS MOST FUNDAMENTAL FORM IS THE ENVIRONMENT WHERE THE BATTLE BETWEEN YOUR LIGHT AND DARK TAKES PLACE

In Reason 2, I also touched on the Dark and Light (one's mind and spirit). What I didn't mention are the allies that both will have in the battle between the two. Reason 0 was about recognising that there is a terrain. This section is about identifying which weapons the light and dark utilise in this battle. Reason 2 was preparation for this point.

EXERCISE #41: TERRAIN REPORT [WB PG 103]

From doing this I realised what parts of my terrain were feeding into my light and what parts were feeding into my dark. I also felt better knowing that there was much room for improvement when it came to my terrain. I felt more in control of my own destiny and it was reassuring knowing that I don't have to feel like a victim to my terrain, but rather I can shape it, so long as I'm aware of what it is.

This felt like identifying two armies going to war and analysing the weapons on either side

- 25 -
ACCEPTING YOUR LIGHT & YOUR DARK

"As far as we can discern, the sole purpose human existence is to kindle a light of meaning in the darkness of mere being"

Carl Jung

If your journey to changing your lifestyle goes anything like mine, you'll realise that doing so will amplify your light, and in particular your dark. To be better able to change my lifestyle I had to learn to accept both sides and that one can't be minimised overnight.

If you went through Reason Zero, you should have a clear idea of what success means to you. With this section of the book being concerned with how to adjust one's lifestyle to maximise the chances of success, the terrain can often make that process easier or more difficult. Whilst the terrain is your environment, your definition of success should be seen as a journey with many pit stops, which I also like to call milestones. When having a clear idea of what success is to me, I experienced feeling inner resistance. This inner resistance I have felt all my life. This was definitely coming from my dark. I was deemed lazy by almost all my teachers from school all the way through to university.

Lazy is ironically the most lazy word to use when describing someone because there are so many layers to why someone would 'appear' lazy that it should be recognised as something deeper. I always felt like I was destined for great things and I would have great ideas to help make it happen. I however would feel like I was holding myself back. Throughout my childhood, I was constantly labelled as lazy and I can understand why. I would procrastinate like it was a religion, as well as daydreaming, doing things last minute, avoiding tasks all together, and if I 'had' to do something, minimising the effort that I put in. The biggest problem wasn't that I was doing it, it was the fact that I **actually enjoyed doing it**. It felt good playing video games when I should be working on an assignment for example. It felt like I was fighting an internal struggle that I didn't fully know was going on

What I didn't accept though is this...

THERE IS A PART OF YOU THAT WANTS TO BE SUCCESSFUL, AND THERE IS A PART OF YOU THAT WANTS THINGS TO STAY EXACTLY THE SAME'

The part of you that wants you to be successful is your light, and the other part of you that wants things to stay exactly as they are is your dark. Both your light and dark are leaders and the terrain can and will serve either one of them.

YOUR LIGHT

Your Light is your spirit. The person who you believe deep down you are meant to become. The fundamental emotion behind your spirit is Love. It transcends the terrain and this is where your dreams and aspirations come from. As a result the terrain can change and adapt around your light

YOUR DARK

Your dark is your mind and it's a manifestation of who you were but also who you may consider yourself to be, right now. The fundamental emotion behind your spirit is Fear. It imprisons you to the terrain, with the notion that it can never be changed. The journey to success I thought was determined by how well you manage the terrain, but the terrain is only the battlefield...

175

THE JOURNEY TO SUCCESS IS DETERMINED BY HOW WELL YOUR SPIRIT AND MIND WORK TOGETHER

More specifically its determined by;

-   Your ability to determine what in your terrain feeds your light and what feeds your dark
-   Your ability to feed your light more than your dark
-   Your ability to use your dark to feed your light

I had to realise that slow and small change will always beat no change. There was more value to knocking 1 brick out of a 1 mile high wall, than doing nothing. Doing nothing can feel so easy compared to knocking down one brick. It's easy to think that knocking over one brick won't do anything and we simply either do nothing or knock down the whole wall in one sitting. Your dark is supposed to compel you to act.

THE PURPOSE OF YOUR DARK IS TO SIGNIFY WHEN LIGHT IS REQUIRED, NOT HOW MUCH

The problem is we too often misinterpret this message, so if we feel a brick wall is holding us back, we feel we have to knock it down, and our response is based on whether we feel we can do it or not straight away. So what is the answer? To chip away at it. Gradual change will always beat no change and will most definitely beat drastic change if drastic change appears quickly and disappears just as quickly.

So how can we start adding gradual change to help us in our journey to feeding our light and using the dark to feed the light? Simply by having morning and evening routines.

MORNING ROUTINES

For the sake of simplicity and getting things started, I'll define a morning routine as what you do within the first two hours of waking up. This has often been highly recommended by successful people who will swear by the benefits of having a morning routine. It can quite literally help you to mould your day by starting off as you mean to go along. And due to the power of the internet, you can even find the morning routines of super successful people.

Some great elements of a good morning routine are:

- Early Wake Up Time (at the same time every day, and yes that includes weekends)
- Exercise
- One of your most difficult tasks that day (or a task that you very reluctant to do)
- Doing something that means the most to you
- Mental Relaxation/Preparation (e.g. Meditating)
- Any other activity that sharpens your focus

NB: You can do this by searching online "Successful People Morning Routines' and try out a few to see what works for you.

EVENING ROUTINES

Following the same logic as morning routines, an evening routine is what you do 1-2hrs before you go to bed. Having an evening routine is one of the best ways to improve your quality of sleep. It's not too difficult to get a certain amount of sleep in terms of hours but quality is much more important. Ever got 8 hours of sleep but still feel tired? 8 hrs would be considered a great number of hours for sleep for the average adult, but that alone doesn't guarantee that the mind, body and spirit will be fully rested.

It is actually recommended that you detach yourself from any technology or device that can emit radiation (even at a small level, like blue light) for at least 1hr before you go to bed. The idea of the evening routine is to wind your body down from the intense day to day activity to get you prepared for sleep.

Some elements of a good evening routine are:

- Bed Time: (ideally at the same time every day, including weekends)
- Reflection (of your day/week/month/year)
- Planning (next day/week/month/year/etc)
- Detaching from Technology (e.g. phone and computer)
- Cleaning
- Reading
- Mental Relaxation (e.g. meditating)
- Any other activity that makes it easier to fall asleep.

EXERCISE #42: MORNING ROUTINE [WB PG 109]

EXERCISE #43: EVENING ROUTINE [WB PG 110]

- 26 -
ATTACHMENT MANAGEMENT: WHAT'S A FAIR TRADE TO YOU?

"A young woman lives, an old man dies, fair trade"

Detective John Hartigan, Sin City (2005)

Attachments are what make us human, it can propel us forward but it can also be the very thing that is holding us back. The reason why I've called this chapter Attachment Management rather than 'Letting Go of Attachments' is because not all attachments are bad for you and it's good to recognise the difference between healthy and unhealthy attachments. The challenge is to become aware of your attachments and then identify which ones are assets and which ones are liabilities.

This is even more of a challenge because discerning which of your attachments or assets and which ones are liabilities is relative to your definition of success, e.g.Your attachment to playing video games is an asset if your definition of success is to be a professional esports gamer, but it may become a liability if you want to an owner of a pencil manufacturing company. Also the reality of this is the fact that as you uncover layers to your definition of success, or redefine it completely, what were once attachment assets can now become liabilities and vice versa.

ATTACHMENTS ARE DIFFICULT TO LET GO OF BECAUSE WE OFTEN DEFINE OURSELVES BY THEM, AND ASSOCIATE LETTING THEM GO WITH DEATH

I've noticed within myself and others that the deeper our attachment is of something or someone, the closer we link it to our self identity. The reason we do the things we do so often is because we define that as who we are. As an example, let me present two people who both smoke.

Matthew: "I smoke"
William: "I am a smoker"

Who of the two do you think has a deeper attachment to smoking? You would be right in thinking it was William. Part of the recovery process for addiction is to detach one's identity from the activity that they are trying to no longer do. I was truly attached to my expectations and assumptions. I've already mentioned expectations in Reason 2 and assumptions in Reason 3. To further add to my previous thoughts, I discovered on this journey that expectations and assumptions don't just appear from thin air. So how did it come about? This is how I see it

Experience & Environment >>>>> Interpretation >>>>> Expectations & Assumptions

You can't control what happens to you, but you can control your philosophy (what you choose to interpret your experiences). So with that being said, it's easy to see that my attachment to my 'philosophy' will then be a massive influence on my expectations and assumptions.

My previous philosophy was that expectations and assumptions were the cornerstone of my intelligence. I thought the purpose of my expectations were to serve as my standards, and the purpose of my assumptions was to protect me from the negative side of the world. What ended up happening was that my expectations served as a maximum security prison I could never get out of, and my assumptions served as the spiritual friend who can convince you to never try and feel smarter than everyone else for it. Doing my diet and terrain report made me aware of the many unhealthy and healthy attachments I had made and many of them I can recall struggling to truly detach myself from. So how did I overcome this problem? The answer may be simple to say but it is far more difficult to implement.

THE BEST WAY TO DETACH FROM UNHEALTHY HABITS IS TO DO SO IN STAGES, SLOWLY AND GRADUALLY, RATHER THAN BY A GREAT LEAP

My mistake with trying to make lifestyle changes was that I tried to do too much too soon. As a result I would get a massive case of withdrawal symptoms/inner resistance and I would end up going back to my old ways. A common saying is that the devil is in the details, I actually disagree with that sentiment...

POWER IS IN THE DETAILS, THAT'S WHY THE DEVIL'S THERE

It is better to do a little over a long period of time, than a lot over a short period of time. You ask any big corporation as to whether they would rather get a lump sum of money from you in one day or to take a little from you over your lifetime, and you may be surprised that the majority of them would take a little over your lifetime. The reason why is because of concepts like compound interest, where consistency is truly rewarded and they would receive a whole lot more money from you than if you just paid a lump sum there and then. Going to an example of eating junk food in a poor diet, here is a common attempt of severing an attachment

2 Bars of Chocolate>>>>>>>> An Apple (or other fruit)

181

Even though this example is replacing something sweet with something that is sweet, this may not be a jump that is comfortable (as there is a different type of sweetness).

A more practical example of severing an attachment can be.

**2 Bars of Chocolate>>>>>>>1 Bar of Chocolate>>>>>>>
Cereal Bar>>>>> An Apple**

This example is by no means designed to win any literary awards, but I'm sure you understand the point I'm making. If you do want to switch straight from 2 bars of chocolate to even carrot sticks, that is great, you just need to find the alternative that you personally enjoy. When I'm working with my clients, we will often assess their current food diet as a metric to gauge their current lifestyle. In the event where a client admits they need to work on, I don't tell them to eat more vegetables, I simply ask them what vegetables they genuinely like. Starting with what you like will always be a better starting place than starting somewhere that is the healthiest. A great attitude to have at the start is to ask yourself what is the step of each change you can make that you feel you could do for the rest of your life.

ALWAYS LOOK FOR THE FAIR TRADE

It can be easy to solely focus on what you are giving up when becoming successful/happy. Countless people on countless occasions will stress the importance of being able to make sacrifices as a prerequisite. I saw sacrifices almost like mini deaths because I was so attached to the things that I felt I would need to sacrifice. That being said, what is more important to identify and focus on is what you would be receiving in return for sacrificing something that you are attached to. The only things that you would consider worth giving up your unhealthy attachments for need to be linked to your definition of success and happiness. Change and action will come soon after any situation where your desire is stronger than your fear (in this case, fear of loss of this unhealthy attachment). You then have a choice as to what is more important to you.

EXERCISE #44: LIFESTYLE ATTACHMENT TRADER [WB PG 111]

When I first did this exercise, it was a challenge for me as I found it difficult to find healthier alternatives that I actually liked the idea of. It was worth the effort though and I noticed slowly but surely my lifestyle changing compared to what it used to be. What made it easier was that for the benefit I was getting from severing these unhealthy attachments outweighed the things about those unhealthy habits that I loved. But this appreciation only happened over time. For every unhealthy attachment, there is always a healthier alternative and stages in which you can transition closer and closer to it. Committing to the lifestyle of subtle yet sustainable change will always win, versus trying to change everything all in one go.

27

TESTING, TESTING: THE FOUNDATION OF ANYTHING THAT ADDS VALUE

"The problem is not that testing is the bottleneck. The problem is that you don't know what's in the bottle"

Michael Bolton

I HATE testing. To me success is doing something right at the FIRST attempt. Anything else is a failure. This has been my current way of doing things...

Thinking -------> Thinking ----------> Thinking -------> Thinking------>
Being forced to do something (due to circumstance) -----> Evaluating
Thinking -------> Planning-----------> Testing (AKA doing) --------> Evaluating

What I didn't realise was that maybe the process of attempting my definition of success was to enjoy the process of attempting rather than the outcomes of failure or success. I say this because I soon realised that I had to see changing my lifestyle as a lifelong journey, rather than seeing it as the destination. Just then I recognised that my definition of success may well end up having multiple layers that reveal themselves after work and time, my life would need to be aligned in line with it. At the same time, only trial and error would be the true way of me uncovering all of these layers. As you're creating your ideal lifestyle, your morning and evening routines may feel great in the moment but you may try them out to realise that you don't like it or it doesn't work for you. A great example is when I started doing this. When it came to my most important tasks/projects, I would spend all of the time worrying about it and procrastinating, just before the last minute where I would work frantically to get it done before the deadline. I tried to force myself to do my most difficult tasks in one sitting later on in the afternoon/stroke evening and that simply didn't work for me. So I tried doing my most difficult tasks earlier in the day and rather than trying to do it in one sitting, I would spread it out and do a little every day, which worked a whole lot better.

YOUR LIFESTYLE DOESN'T PARTICULAR MATTER, AS LONG AS IT IS HEALTHY AND INCREASES YOUR CHANCES OF ACHIEVING YOUR DEFINITION OF SUCCESS

As the saying goes, 'There is more than one way to skin a cat'. Success doesn't have only one path, and the fact that by now you may well have discovered and accepted your definition of success will mean that you will know that your path will be different compared to others (maybe even the ones closest to you who mean the most). The most beautiful thing about life is that many people have got to the same destination using different paths, the most important thing is to find the one that works for you.

Yes you could try Elon Musk's morning routine, but you may find that Oprah Winfrey's morning routine works much better. You can research others' lifestyles and be inspired to put together your own. And that's the bigger part of it all. You can be certain that many of the people you consider successful not only tested other elements of their lives but they mostly enjoy testing, simply because they see the value it brings. The first value I live by and that I brought up earlier in the book was 'To Win Is To Try', the reason why is because...

VALUE #8: THERE IS MORE VALUE IN IMPERFECTION THAN PERFECTION

185

By more value, I mean to us humans (not deities or divine beings). I say this because of a truth I've expressed many times in this book, because we are designed to work better together than apart. If we were perfect, there would be no need to work together and we would miss out on the true enjoyment of life that is sharing it with others.

EXERCISE #45: TRY JOURNAL [WB PG 112]

This exercise has overlap with the Help Journal exercise in Reason 3. An argument could be made that it could have come up earlier in the book, but it's here for a reason. I realised that I focused too much on the small, which is important, but I also needed to think more on the bigger picture. There is no bigger picture than your lifestyle. Yes, tasks and projects are important, but if they don't serve the lifestyle you need to live to reach your definition of success, then it is pointless. At the same time I realised through doing this that the biggest and most positive lifestyle changes that happened were sparked by trying something that I was (often severely) reluctant to try.

So what happens if I try and the outcome isn't the ideal one? Try again and keep trying. The more you try the better you get. If Thomas Edison (who attempted to create the light bulb over 1,000 times) saw his failures 1,000 'failures' as 1,000 steps to the end goal, then what makes you special enough to only succeed after the first try?

The bigger point is to make trying a lifelong habit...

LOVING THE PROCESS MORE THAN AN OUTCOME, WILL GIVE YOU BETTER OUTCOMES, PLURAL

The only question is which process do you like the idea of? And what process do you actually enjoy now that you've tried doing it? Saying how long that process would take for you is like asking how long is a piece of string. It took me a while to get to this point so I won't lie to you and say that it's guaranteed to take a couple of weeks. What I will say though is enjoying the process made the time go quickly.

28

THE LEVELS OF SELF INTEREST

*"You can have everything you want in life if
you will just help enough people get what they want"*

Zig Ziglar

So what happens if there is ever a time when you hit a brick wall when trying to work on your lifestyle? Remember this...

IT'S ALWAYS BETTER TO WORK ON SOMETHING BIT-BY-BIT, THAN NOT AT ALL

There very well may be times when you know what your priority is but you may struggle with it. This can be due to numerous reasons;

- You don't find it interesting
- You need help
- Self doubt/fear.

When this happens, your mind will try and help you avoid this feeling of hitting a brick wall. Common responses included but aren't limited to

- Procrastination
- Avoidance (e.g. looking for and engaging in activities that you do find interesting)

A good thing to do whenever this happens is to ask yourself the following questions and **accept** the honest answer.

1. Do I find this interesting? And Why?
2. Do I need help? And if so, from who?
3. Do I believe I can achieve this?
4. Is there anything that scares me about doing this?

One of the things that you will come across if you were to research and study the successful and what it takes, is they are comfortable answering the above questions and asking themselves this question on a regular basis.

This taps into their levels of self interest. We often have to make choices between our different levels of self interest as the different levels of our self interest can conflict with each other. Similar to sacrifices, these choices can be subjective but in essence choosing the medium and long term over the short term consists of choosing against doing something you **probably really want to do**. Seeing it as such made it even easier for me to make these choices, whether it's waking up early in the morning when you really want to stay in and sleep a few more hours or even saying no to something you'd really enjoy in the short term, to instead do something that you'll enjoy in the medium and longer term.

In short, most human beings may never achieve success because

YOU WILL PROBABLY ALWAYS WANT TO CHOOSE THE SHORT TERM OVER THE MEDIUM AND LONG TERM

A lot of successful people will agree with this and may go further to say that they overcame their desire to choose the short term by either willpower, self discipline or a grander vision of what they truly wanted to accomplish. Yes, whilst having a clear definition of success will help you in choosing the long term over the short term, I'd argue that you won't choose the long term over the short term long enough for you to see solid and long standing results.

So what's the answer you say?...

VALUE #9: LOVE THE PROCESS MORE THAN THE OUTCOME

The truth is that for you to truly become your definition of successful. You are going to need to fall in love with the process of becoming successful rather than the 'end product'. And the reason is simple.

IF YOU SEE BECOMING SUCCESSFUL AS A PAINFUL JOURNEY AND SUCCESS AS A BEAUTIFUL DESTINATION. YOU WILL LIVE MORE OF YOUR LIFE IN PAIN, THAN EXPERIENCING ITS BEAUTY

And who truly wants to live a life of pain?, especially when they may not have a real idea of how long the journey is going to be until they reach this 'destination'. The quicker you fall in love with the process, the more likely you are going to become successful/happy.

So the question is. How do I fall in love with the process? Whilst I was working in a fundraising company I had an issue with my line manager. With that being said, I was on talking terms with a lot of the people within the company. From high level managers, to even the directors and founders of the company. On one occasion I caught one of the directors (by the name of Angela Marie Graham. She had a fierce reputation, to the point that she was called AMG, but she was great with me, almost like a work Aunt) and we were having a general conversation when I asked her how I could get my line manager to understand and subscribe to my perspective of how to improve things. Her advice was a game changer...

WHEN YOU WANT TO PERSUADE SOMEONE (YOURSELF INCLUDED), OF ANYTHING, SPEAK TO THEIR SELF INTEREST

The key to this is to understand what is important to someone. If you are asking someone to do something, whether or not they do it will depend on whether they feel that doing so will bring value to them in relation to what matters to them or what they are interested in. From that moment I realised that I was only communicating to people from the vantage point that they should do it because... 'it is the right thing to do' or 'because I'm smart and I'm right on this one'.

I got a little bit better at persuasion but I still wasn't quite where I wanted to be. At this point I was trying to even persuade myself to take certain actions. Human beings often know what is right or wrong to do, but how many of us still do the 'wrong' thing. Whether it's eating unhealthy food when you are supposed to be on a diet, to watching TV when you know you should be working.

Most people's motivation to do something is normally the vision of the outcome. Doing a bucket list and vision board is great for helping with this, however it's incomplete advice because alone it can help you focus too much on the outcome. After much reflection I realised that I truly didn't understand self interest. To understand self interest is to understand that there are levels to it. I've pretty much alluded to them already in this chapter, but I'll emphatically state that these are:

1. Short Term
2. Medium Term
3. Long Term

It's truly important to understand these three levels of self interest within yourself, but also within others. The reason why is because whenever you communicate with them and ask them for something (including yourself) you should be able to explain how doing so can appeal to **<u>all three</u>** levels of self interest (or whichever one(s) they care more about)

TO ACHIEVE THE OUTCOME(S) YOU DESIRE, YOU ARE PROBABLY GOING TO HAVE TO GO THROUGH THE PROCESS LONGER THAN YOU THOUGHT YOU WOULD

For anyone to enjoy any process, it has to serve their short term and medium term self interests. This is another reason why all three levels of self interest should be in harmony. Your goals will often cater to your long term self interest but if your medium term and short term self interests aren't in harmony with your long term self interest, then you are going to struggle.

E..g - Getting a six pack

Short Term Self Interest - Eating whatever I feel like
Medium Term - Exercise when I feel like it
Long Term - Getting a six pack

I had to ask myself, "How much of my time do I spend on pursuing my definition of success?' and the answer was nowhere near enough. Now this could be because I'm not truly pursuing my definition of success but also it could be that I need to better link my three levels of self interest. Your 3 levels of self interest not only can change from time to time but it can also be different in relation to the situation. Your three levels of self interest in your family life might be different to your three levels of self interest at work. My three levels of self interest for the most part are.

1. Short Term - Feel freedom & peace of mind
2. Do what I want to do
3. Achieve financial freedom

You may not notice, but there is conflict within these three levels. If I feel free all the time and do what I want to do, will I achieve financial freedom? The answer is most probably not and this conflict is commonly why people don't achieve their goals. So what is the answer? You almost need to see each level of your self interest as a separate person and the answer is to identify how each level of your self interest will be taken care of.

A small example might in regards to doing an assignment in college

"The quicker I get this assignment done the quicker I'll feel free and because I really don't want to do this assignment I'm going to feel even more freedom and peace of mind when I'm finished. This gives me more time to do what I want to do, which is playing games online. And doing this more often is going to help me achieve financial freedom, where I'll get to do what I want to do for most of my life, rather than waiting for retirement. Seems like a fair trade"

EXERCISE #46: LEVELS OF SELF INTEREST [WB PG 113]

Doing this revealed to me how much my short term and long term interests weren't aligned, but at the same time what it meant was I had to align my lifestyle changes with some of my short term interests to make it easier to make the changes. An example of this is my short term interest for instant gratification (which alone will derail my chances of success). To satisfy my short term interests I created a culture of rewarding myself whenever I completed a process of some sort. This helped me create a culture of constant processes that I enjoy, but also a culture of regularly rewarding myself so that I got a taste of the instant satisfaction that I like. Over time your levels of self interest may even change, where your short term level of self interest becomes something more profound (e.g. going from instant gratification to helping someone else). With that being said, it is important to align your lifestyle changes to all three levels of self interest.

During this journey however, what started to happen was I would forget to reward myself and would just continue with my lifestyle changes until I hit a brick wall. I noted that this was because at the time I didn't have a significant amount of things to reward myself with. Similarly to how a diet can stall because there is not enough variety of food options and just like a fitness plan can stall because there is not enough variety of exercises and lack of cross training. Humans are conditioned to respond to variety because the mind, body and spirit will get used to the same pattern of behaviour. It is why in the world of fitness, it's recommended to do different forms of training throughout the year. What I needed was a list of things that I would consider a reward for my behaviour & choices, which could serve my levels of self interest. I created a reward list of things that catered to my short term interests most and a happiness list of things that catered to my medium and long term happiness. The reward list was more to reward the past version of me that was still attached to old and unhelpful behaviours and the happiness list was more about what made me happy in the present moment.

EXERCISE #47: REWARD LIST [WB PG 114]

EXERCISE #48: HAPPINESS LIST [WB PG 115]

This created a very much needed emotional, mental and spiritual lubrication to my journey to align my lifestyle to my definition of success. Many of the things on the happiness list ironically increased my chances of success (e.g. such as watching an inspiring documentary). Just because your old lifestyle wasn't fully aligned with your chances of success, doesn't mean that everything about it necessarily has to go (with the exception of anything that puts you or anyone else in danger).

29

PRODUCTIVITY: TIPS TO RUN YOUR LIFE RATHER THAN HAVE IT RUNNING YOU

"Either you run the day, or the day runs you"

Jim Rohn

When working on aligning my lifestyle to my definition of success, I realised that I have a tendency to over invest my time and energy into the things that are important to me. I would often take a few hours on something that I could get done in 1hr. As a result of this I would neglect other things that were important for me for the sake of the one thing at the time that I would consider important. This of course was prone to change and the changes would happen based on how I felt, rather than any rhyme or reason. I had to reconcile however that doing this was damaging my chances of achieving my definition of success. The energy I would invest would often have me feeling drained.

This started a lengthy and even now an ongoing journey of improving my time effectiveness. The best way to honour this concept would be to make this chapter short and share with you the different tactics that worked for me when it came to productivity.

SELF- IMPOSED DEADLINES

In school, I hated deadlines with an intense passion. What I disliked about it was I didn't like being told what to do (I still don't to be fair). I felt restricted and even oppressed by them. What I didn't understand though was not only its value, but its value to my pursuit of success. Then I found a way to exploit its value and stick to my rebelliousness…

ALWAYS HAVE AN INTERNAL DEADLINE THAT IS EARLIER THAN ANY EXTERNAL DEADLINE YOU'VE BEEN SET

If you have any assignment due in two weeks, get it done 1 week early. If someone asks you to get something to them within 48hrs, then aim to give it to them within 24 hours. What is better is when you don't even tell them your self imposed deadline and you just deliver by then.

This adds benefit for many reasons. For one, it helps you underpromise and over deliver (a quality that you will be loved for in all forms of your life, believe me). Another being that it helps foster self confidence and even a level of power and control in your own destiny. The final one being that it gives you margin of error, which is great when dealing with potential worst case scenarios.

T.T.L - TO TRY LIST

Everyone has heard of the to do list and it was something I would be obsessed over. I realised though that I would develop anxiety over these types of lists because I would feel like a failure if they weren't all completed. To make matters worse I would avoid starting altogether if I didn't feel like I could complete it. What really worked for me was changing it to a to try list and this one of the best ways to honour my value that to win is to try.. This means that I could tick off the item on the list the second I attempted it (Note: An attempt would consist of spending at least 3 minutes on the task). As a result I would start a lot earlier and would even get more work done.

M.V.T - MOST VALUABLE TASK

Every evening I would identify what was the task that would bring me the most value. Previously I would only prioritise tasks on what would take me

196

the longest to complete. What I soon realised was that a lot of the most valuable tasks didn't often take that long, it was just the mental/emotional or even spiritual challenge of doing them that would cause me to overthink them and thus waste time. Getting them done during my most productive time of day (early mornings) was an absolute game changer. There are certain tasks now that I only do in the mornings and if I don't, I wait until the next day

POMODOROS

This is a technique where you identify a task that you want to do and you focus on it for a set period of time like nothing in your life matters or even exists. One session of the chosen set time is called one pomodoro and the aim is to complete a certain amount of pomodoros per day. The duration for how long you do this depends on how long you can concentrate for. I started off 25mins at a time, but by all means experiment with what duration works for you (e.g. 5mins, 10mins, 25mins,etc). Additionally, trying to increase the amount of pomodoros you do during the day can maximise your productivity. This technique can help develop a high level of focus and it's great for conditioning yourself to not respond to distractions. This technique is proof that single tasking (only focusing on one task at a time) makes you more effective than multitasking. A great book that goes even further into this concept is called Deep Work by Cal Newport

FREEDOM SPRINT

This exercise is something I came up with to improve my balance, in the sense of getting a lot of things done, across different categories in my life. The purpose of this is to identify 5 tasks that you wish to get done in a day, and spend at least 1 minute on each task. Of course, you won't be able to get any of the tasks completed, but the point of this is to get better at switching in between tasks across a day. This was a massive one for me because I would often have five things I needed to get done and end up spending most of it on item number one, rather than making time and sticking to the time commitment so that I could cater to all five. As you get more and more confident you can increase the intervals by 1-5 minute increments. For you to make this exercise work, you will need an interval timer (which you can get by downloading one on your smartphone. You can even create one online via the following website…

https://www.intervaltimer.com/create/hiit-timer
An interval will ring after every interval (in this case 1minute),
which is great for reminding you when you need to switch tasks.

ACCOUNTABILITY BUDDIES/PARTNERS

This one was and still is a game changer for me. This concept consists of having a goal, a deadline and asking someone else to hold you accountable to that goal and deadline. This person can be someone you trust or some-one who's opinion/approval you hold in high regard. I did mention earlier in the book that pursuing someone else's approval is unhealthy, however, as there are exceptions to every rule, this is the one exception to the rule. Ironically, the more you value the approval of your accountability partner, the more effective this technique will be. Doing this also combined my need to improve my trust issues with others when it came to making life-style changes that better aligned me with my definition of success. This technique is actually one of the biggest factors in me being able to finish the book. Having an accountability partner works best if you set a goal and have mini goals (or milestones) to be working towards with regular review dates. I would be lying if I said that I didn't do a lot of work last minute before an accountability deadline/ review, but the point is that having review dates in the first place resulted in me being far more productive.

OSMOSIS - SURROUNDING SELF WITH PRODUCTIVE PEOPLE

If there is one thing I would want you to get from this chapter, and the whole book for that matter, is the importance of Osmosis. Your lifestyle should consist of surrounding yourself with the type of people that you wish to become like on a regular basis. In this example, surrounding yourself with productive people will make you more productive. Truly successful people not only learn to be comfortable with those that are smarter than them, they make a concerted effort to find and surround themselves with those types of people.

Productivity is an artform and from this you may end up coming up with some productivity ideas of your own, what matters is that you become more and more productive.

SO HOW DO I PULL ALL THIS TOGETHER?

You can do this by following the Habituals that are at the end of each section in the. These are designed to turn the suggested work from just exercises to be done once and never again, to things that are done on a regular basis and form part of your new lifestyle. These are just habituals that I came up with so you are free to create your own. The most important thing is that you have things that you do on a regular basis as part of your lifestyle so that the change is permanent rather than temporary.

EXERCISE #49: LIFESTYLE 2.0 [WB PG 116]

The final exercise that I did in this journey was to ask myself what success meant to me having gone through all of this. All you need to do is continue reading to discover my answers but if you want to do it yourself, here are the questions that I asked myself at the conclusion of this journey.

EXERCISE #50: POST QUESTIONNAIRE [WB PG 119]

GROUND FOUR - HABITUALS

1. **Weekly Life Assessment** – Do Weekly
2. **Diet** – Review weekly
3. **Terrain Report** - Review on a monthly basis (last week of month)
4. **Morning & Evening Routine** - Review on a monthly basis
5. **Try Journal**- Do on a weekly basis
6. **Reward & Happiness List (Review)** – Monthly Basis (2nd week of the month)
7. **Lifestyle 2.0** – Monthly basis (last week of the month)

NB: Timings of month are simply a guide, but feel free to change if it doesn't work for you.

30

GRAND OPENING, GRAND CLOSING: FINAL THOUGHTS

My Truth

*This book and this journey for me was about developing a deeper understanding of Love and Fear. It is said that all human action derives from one of these two foundational emotions and for me one of the most fundamental elements of love is acceptance. I had to accept that my definition of success sets me on a different path from others and. I had to accept my true self as the strongest weapon to forge my success and happiness, rather than believing it to be the obstacle. I had to accept that who I am is measured by BOTH the ups and downs of life, not one or the other. I also had to accept that there are processes and systems behind everything in life and respecting those is actually how you can enjoy your life even more, rather than feeling a prisoner of it. I had to accept that life is a more beautiful experience when you choose to trade, rather than feeling that you **have** to trade under duress. The most difficult thing I had to accept though was other people as they are. I would feel bitter and jaded whenever I felt hurt by others, as well as taking it all too personally when it happened. However, what I had to accept was that nobody is perfect, people can be who they are (good, bad or indifferent) and still be of value*

*Acceptance is the **first** step towards true change and even though there are decisions and actions I regret, if I hold onto those regrets I won't be able to use the present moment to realise how those regrets were meant to make me a better person. I would spend a massive majority of my time either fixated on the past or the future, which gets in the way of the present moment where I can really make changes. I now understand whilst writing this book why a lot of successful people don't really have regrets. The reason is because they already used their previous regrets to make themselves who they are presently.*

I didn't truly accept my definition of success because I didn't accept my own spirit and sense of direction, instead having more faith in others' sense of direction. I didn't truly accept myself because I defined myself by my flaws, rather than BOTH my strengths and flaws. I didn't accept my 'It' because it would have meant admitting that I wasn't as perfect as I felt I had to be to deserve success and happiness. I didn't accept the process and systems behind life because I felt like I was too good to follow them (a contradiction if there ever was one). I didn't accept others because I didn't truly let go of my hurt from those past experiences. I would define them by all the bad things they had done to me, rather than both the bad and good.

A big part of doing that was to accept my past. All the decisions I made, all the memories I hold onto and all the habits that I internalised as part of my self image. What I hadn't understood is that accepting the past versions of myself is what would help me become the person I truly wanted to be...

YOU DON'T NEED TO FOLLOW SOMEONE ELSE'S PATH

YOU DON'T HAVE TO BE PERFECT

YOU DON'T NEED TO HAVE FAITH IN YOUR ABILITY TO DEAL WITH LIFE RIGHT THIS SECOND

OTHER PEOPLE DON'T HAVE TO PROVIDE THE PERFECT HELP...

BECAUSE YOU ARE ALREADY WORTHY & YOU ALREADY DESERVE YOUR DEFINITION OF SUCCESS. YOU JUST NEED TO GO FOR IT!!!

NB: If this book has helped you in anyway, or if there is any feedback (good, bad or indifferent), I'd be truly grateful to hear from you. Feel free to contact me via email (contact@emmillio.com)

EPILOGUE:
NOW THIS BOOK IS FINISHED, WHO AM I?

"Yesterday I was clever, so I wanted to change the world.
Today I am wise, so I am changing myself"

Rumi

"I am now a lifestyle and mindset coach, doing the work and delivering value to people across a wide range of ages and generations all across the UK. I have never received as many opportunities as I am currently and I'm enjoying the process of living, connecting with and serving others. I'm 32 years old (soon turning 33) and I've never felt clearer about my purpose and my definition(vision) of success. I've honestly never felt better and clearer headed. The mental idea that I need to be perfect to be good enough or deserve my definition of success is minimised to such a degree that it doesn't affect my life anywhere near what it would before. It's still there, but it doesn't stop me from living the life that I want. I've grown to understand that everything that comes my way, from challenges, to difficult relationships, is designed to help me achieve my definition of success (it is just for me to figure how so).

As all humans, I experience fear and self doubt (even including the severe doubt that anyone would even read this book) but my response to it now is ... "So What?". To further expand on this change in perspective, I am not my thoughts or emotions (even though my thoughts and emotions may try to convince me otherwise) and I work because I enjoy the process. Also, what if my thoughts and emotions are wrong? I've experienced countless times situations where I was convinced with every fibre in my being that it would go one way, and was very pleasantly surprised to see that it went another way. It would be a crying shame if I continued my past thought process of not bothering to try because I believed in my self-doubt, which has proved to be wrong before. To even compound the point, I truly misunderstood the whole point of self-doubt. The purpose of self doubt is actually to help you improve as a person. The fearful and doubting part of myself I use to help me with contingency planning. With that being said though, it is important to believe in your ability to deal with the unknown, and I have never felt more confident in that regard. Where I previously felt like everything would need to be planned to the minute detail. I'm now ok with going out and just trying something.

During this journey I completely forgave the older parts of myself for the grievances I had. From the regrets of the opportunities I didn't take because of fear and doubt, to my responses to past situations. What made it easier to forgive was the fact that without those things I wouldn't be writing this book, and this is one of the greatest achievements of my entire life. Even if no-one reads it, this book has helped me truly change as a person and that for me is more than enough. Anyone else who reads this book will be cherries on top of the already beautiful cake. Through this journey I realised that I was holding onto a lot of past trauma and hurt and was brought up to not trust others, but letting go made me feel a lot lighter spiritually, never mind emotionally and mentally. The journey of writing this book, and then getting this book to your hands (or your eyes if you are reading the digital version of this book, or ears if you are listening to the audio book) wouldn't have been possible without the army of people I've had to learn to trust. I'm by no means the finished article but I don't have to be and I'm living a great life

I can't even believe that I've finished this book. Once before, this book was a valid excuse/story that I would tell others to convince myself that I was truly doing something, but in the beginning, I didn't pursue it like it was something that I was truly serious about. I was so fixated on trying to change and help others but what I didn't realise was how many people's lives I've already improved just by focusing on trying to help myself. With my life coaching frame-work, called VGVR (Vision, Goals, Values & Rituals), I was my first client and the framework that has helped so many people with their own lives first helped me. Every single exercise that is in the book I have actually completed myself and the reason why I can walk so tall and talk so proud about this book is because it truly changed me. It's why it's taken 2 plus years (almost three) to get done. The book was intended to be a book that I could write exactly as I was, without changing. But then it became a different book because I wanted to personify what this book was always about...self transformation.

This may be the start of a new chapter in my journey, it may be the end, who knows? I'm just going to continue enjoying life and let the chapters to my story continue to write themselves... "

APPENDIX

A - THE BLUEPRINT TO SUCCESS:
(READ THIS IF YOU'VE ONLY GOT 5 MINS)

"Would you like me to give you a formula for success? It's quite simple, really: Double your rate of failure. You are thinking of failure as the enemy of success. But it isn't at all. You can be discouraged by failure or you can learn from it, so go ahead and make mistakes. Make all you can. Because remember that's where you will find success."

Thomas J. Watson

If you were to ask me what makes me qualified to even speak on this subject, my answer will be...

"The vast number of books and ebooks I have in my house on the subject"

I have read tons of information on this, to the point where I have given advice to others on how to be successful (the audacity). What I've noticed is a path that if everyone followed (including myself), success would be guaranteed.

Side Note: This blueprint assumes you know what your definition of success is.

1. Habitually Visualise success (via meditation)
2. Seek opportunities to meet and build relationships with people who are ALREADY 'successful'
3. Ask those people to mentor you (until at least one says yes)
4. With the help of those relationships and research, tailor your life routine to match the life routine of the people who are where you want to be.

Without a shadow of a doubt if you follow these five steps you will be successful. I have no doubt about it in my mind. This of course is far easier said than done. Let's go through each one.

1. Habitually visualise success
No book I've read better explains visualising success than The Secret, by Rhonda Bryne. This arguably is the most critically acclaimed book that discusses the law of attraction. For those of you who don't know, the Law of Attraction is a universal law that suggests that whatever we focus on is what we will attract. When visualising, it is important to engage as many of your senses as possible, from imagining the sounds, to the colours, to even the smells (e.g. driving in your dream car)

2. Seek opportunities to meet and build relationships with people who are ALREADY 'successful'
Doing this will help you dramatically because relationships can help you navigate the overwhelming amount of information out there and sift through the high quality opportunities from the low quality one. An important element to this is expressing to others your goals and dreams as you'll soon find that people may know others who can help and offer to introduce you (which wouldn't have happened if you kept your dreams to yourself)

3. Ask those people to mentor you (until at least one says yes)
The value of having a mentor is immeasurable. It will save you time, improve your self confidence and also your chances of success.

4. With the help of those relationships and research, tailor your life routine to match the life routine of the people who are where you want to be.
Having the information is one thing, knowing the right people is another,

and committing your lifestyle to your vision of success is the final step. Going through these steps is also a great way of finding out whether or not it truly is your vision for success. This path isn't for the faint hearted but it has shown to work time and again during human history.

B - HOW TO DISCOVER
AND CREATE OPPORTUNITY

The short answer is as follows...

SHAKE TREES FOR THE FRUIT TO FALL ON YOUR LAP

The trees are relationships & communities. The fruit are opportunities. I could leave it here, but let's first discuss what an opportunity actually is.

Opportunity: *a time or set of circumstances that makes it possible to do something*

So what kind of circumstance or situation can be seen as an opportunity?...

ANY AND EVERY SITUATION THAT CAN INCREASE YOUR CHANCES OF ACHIEVING A DESIRED/POSITIVE OUTCOME

It couldn't be any more simpler than that. The more you are in tune with your definition of success, the easier it is for you to discover and recognise opportunities when they come. To better discover opportunities, it is only half the battle to know their nature (due to the fact that a significant number of people can often mistake an opportunity for a problem). The next step is to understand what type of opportunities would increase your chances of the desired outcome (in this case your definition of success). One situation can be a problem to someone and the same exact situation can be a golden opportunity to someone else. The only reason there is a difference is because those two individuals have two different definitions of success. This philosophy greatly helped me change the way I saw opportunities.

WHAT IF EVERY SITUATION YOU WENT THROUGH AND WILL GO THROUGH WAS PREPARED OPPORTUNITIES, GIVEN BY (INSERT DEITY YOU BELIEVE IN HERE) AND/OR THE UNIVERSE TO HELP YOU ACHIEVE YOUR DEFINITION OF SUCCESS?

That may well change your perspective a lot. We often feel like victims whenever we encounter a situation we consider negative. But if we see it differently and more like something that is designed to help, we'd be more likely to see ourselves as superheroes who have been shown the villain's weak spot(s) during our 'showdown'. This change in perspective will help you with the next step: identifying the ideal opportunities for your desired definition of success. Yes fruit may fall on your lap, but they may not be the right fruit. Starting off, you probably won't know the difference so explore all that falls on your lap (unless advised otherwise by a mentor). As you continue the journey, you will cultivate your own instincts, which may at times go against any mentors you have (mentors aren't right all of the time, most often than not) Another thing to discuss are the trees. Are you shaking the right ones? You can't be angry if you are shaking mango trees and having mangoes fall on your lap, when you are looking for apples. Understanding what fruit you want makes it easier to discover the right trees to shake. I'll speak for myself when I say that I've spent a lot of my life shaking the wrong trees. Some that would bear the wrong fruit, and some that don't have any leaves whatsoever, never mind fruit. The best source of opportunities in my life experience has been other people. I will definitely say I've been blessed to have met and built relationships with many people in life who are always aware of the best trees to shake and extend opportunities to me.

As mentioned in the beginning, the answer to this question is to shake trees, but what questions would help you discover and create these opportunities?

Here is a non exhaustive list that is a good starting point:

Discovering and Creating Opportunities (For Yourself)
- What do I want? (already covered in REASON 0)
- What are the types of opportunities for me to do what I want?
- Who is most likely to know where the opportunities are?
- How can I help those who are most likely to know where the opportunities are?
- Where are the opportunities most likely to be?
- Which community(s) will make opportunities easier to come across?
- How can I serve those community(s)?
- What preparation do I need to do to be ready to exploit opportunities?

Discovering and Creating Opportunities (For Others)
- What do I want?
- What can I get help & support with?
- Who can I approach for help and where can I find them?
- How can I publicly ask for help?
- How can I share an opportunity that I've discovered?
- Who would benefit from an opportunity I've discovered?

These questions will help you determine what types of fruit you want, and subsequently determine the type of trees you should be shaking (for example, there would be not any point building a relationship with a bricklayer in Leeds if you want to work as a forensic scientist in London)

THE BEST OPPORTUNITY(S) CAN COME AT THE WORST TIME(S)

This is especially true in the creative industries (e.g. music/film/entertainment), where competition is high and there are more people than opportunities. It is important to bear this in mind, as one's chances of success is greatly affected by one's readiness to take advantage of an opportunity. The biggest problem when looking to discover and create opportunity is the bigger the perceived risk, the greater the desire for a guaranteed outcome. If you don't foresee the ideal outcome to be guaranteed, this may influence you to not take this perceived risk. This attitude is nothing short of naive and is something that can greatly impede you. It's naive because it would require you to make child-like assumptions, such as the assumption that any failure wouldn't have any added benefit to and increase your chances of success.

C - SUCCESS CHECKLIST

REASON ZERO

- ☐ PRE QUESTIONNAIRE
- ☐ BUCKET LIST
- ☐ BUCKET LIST QUESTIONNAIRE
- ☐ VISION BOARD
- ☐ BUCKET LIST MENU
- ☐ THE VISION

REASON ONE

- ☐ PERFECTIONIST QUESTIONNAIRE
- ☐ PERSONAL RIGHTS QUESTIONNAIRE
- ☐ PERSONAL BILL OF RIGHTS
- ☐ I.P.B. CHART
- ☐ GOOD ENOUGH LIST
- ☐ R.O.G.E CHART
- ☐ 'ALREADY DONE' BUCKET LIST
- ☐ BRANCH FINDER
- ☐ L.O.G.E. ASSESSMENT
- ☐ COMPETENCY QUESTIONNAIRE

REASON TWO

- ☐ 'IT' LIST
- ☐ 'IT' MEDITATION
- ☐ INTERNAL SENSE OF SHOULD QUESTIONNAIRE
- ☐ WHY NOT? QUESTIONNAIRE
- ☐ LIGHT VS DARK CONVO
- ☐ VICTIM STORY
- ☐ HERO STORY

REASON THREE

- ☐ HURT LIST
- ☐ FORGIVENESS LETTER
- ☐ VILLAIN LIST
- ☐ APOLOGY LETTER
- ☐ SELF FORGIVENESS LETTER
- ☐ 'SELF MADE' STRESS TEST
- ☐ APPROVAL LIST
- ☐ EXTERNAL SENSE OF SHOULD
- ☐ E.P.B. CHART
- ☐ OP-DNW CHART
- ☐ OP QUESTIONNAIRE
- ☐ HELP LIST
- ☐ HELP JOURNEY

REASON FOUR

- ☐ WEEKLY LIFE ASSESSMENT
- ☐ CURRENT LIFESTYLE MAP
- ☐ FUTURE LIFE FORECAST
- ☐ DIET
- ☐ TERRAIN REPORT
- ☐ MORNING ROUTINE
- ☐ EVENING ROUTINE
- ☐ LIFESTYLE ATTACHMENT TRADER
- ☐ TRY JOURNAL
- ☐ LEVES OF SELF INTEREST
- ☐ REWARD LIST
- ☐ HAPPINESS LIST
- ☐ LIFESTYLE 2.0
- ☐ POST QUESTIONNAIRE

D - NINE VALUES OF WAYSY

1. TO WIN IS TO TRY
2. TREAT YOURSELF THE WAY YOU WANT TO BE TREATED
3. I'M ALREADY GOOD ENOUGH (TO START AT THE VERY LEAST)
4. ACTION BEFORE SELF CONFIDENCE
5. I CAN HANDLE 'IT'
6. 10:90
7. KNOW YOUR LIMITATIONS
8. THERE IS MORE VALUE IN IMPERFECTION THAN PERFECTION
9. LOVE THE PROCESS MORE THAN THE OUTCOME

BIBLIOGRAPHY

Taghavi, Aram Rasa (2017) *Here's why most people aren't successful and how you can ensure you'll succeed*: The Start Up
https://medium.com/swlh/8-reasons-most-people-arent-successful-and-8-ways-to-ensure-you-ll-succeed-7e8be17e5187

Unknown (Unknown) *What is the Law of Attraction? Open your eyes to a world of endless possibilities:* The Law of Attraction.com
http://www.thelawofattraction.com/what-is-the-law-of-attraction/

Tabaka, Marla (2017) *8 Signs You're A Perfectionist (and Why It's Toxic To Your Mental Health),* Inc.
https://www.inc.com/marla-tabaka/8-signs-youre-a-perfectionist-and-why-its-toxic-to-your-mental-health.html

Sabatier, Grant (2018) *I Retired A Millionaire at 30 – and now I know why everyone is so unhappy*: Business Insider
https://www.businessinsider.com/i-retired-a-millionaire-at-30-but-i-now-know-success-isnt-about-money-2018-6/?IR=T

Lalonde, Joseph (2016) *5 Reasons You Aren't Successful*: Success
https://www.success.com/5-reasons-you-arent-successful/

Demers, Jayson (2014) *51 Quotes To Inspire Success In Your Life and Business:* Inc.
https://www.inc.com/jayson-demers/51-quotes-to-inspire-success-in-your-life-and-business.html

Jenika (2016) *Make you fear of success obsolete:* Psychology For Photographers
https://psychologyforphotographers.com/fear-of-success-solutions

Imafidon, Casey (Unknown) *Why People Who Focus More On Processes Than Outcomes Gain More In Their Life:* Lifehack
https://www.lifehack.org/338162/why-people-that-focus-more-process-than-outcomes-get-better-results

Dessi, Chris (2016) *How to get comfortable with being uncomfortable (according to a green beret):* Inc.
https://www.inc.com/chris-dessi/how-to-get-comfortable-with-being-uncomfortable-according-to-a-green-beret.html

Oppong, Thomas (2018) *Make Life Easier on Yourself by Accepting "Good Enough." Don't Pursue Perfection, Pursue Progress:* Medium
https://medium.com/personal-growth/make-life-easier-on-yourself-by-accepting-good-enough-accept-the-lack-of-perfect-5bac47c98ec8

Camera Wilkins, Melissa (Unknown) *What It Means To Be Good Enough:* Melissa Camera Wilkins
https://melissacamarawilkins.com/what-it-means-to-be-enough/#:~:text=Having%20a%20good%20grasp%20on,need%20anyone%20or%20anything%20else.

Adams, Rachael (Unknown) *14 Quotes to Encourage and Inspire Growth:* Journey Strength
https://journeystrength.com/14-quotes-to-encourage-and-inspire-growth/

Gerencer, Tom (2018) *Hard Skills vs Soft Skills: What's the Difference?* : Zety
https://zety.com/blog/hard-skills-soft-skills#:~:text=Hard%20skills%20are%20teachable%20and,getting%20along%20with%20other%20people

Davies, R.J. (Unknown) *Weeds & Trees - Weed control for successful tree establishment:* Forest Research
https://www.forestresearch.gov.uk/documents/6723/FCHB002.pdf

Demers, Jayson (2015) *7 Traits Only Happy People Have:* Inc.
https://www.inc.com/jayson-demers/7-traits-only-happy-people-have.html

Sykes, Timothy (2018) *5 Traits of Successful People:* Entrepreneur
https://www.entrepreneur.com/article/315161

Chesak, Jennifer (2018) *The No BS Guide To Protecting Your Emotional Space:* Healthline
https://www.healthline.com/health/mental-health/set-boundaries?c=355275925550#intro

Unknown (Unknown) *8 Personal Rights Which Are Essential For Quality of Life:* Live Your True Story
https://www.liveyourtruestory.com/8-personal-rights-which-are-essential-for-quality-of-life-communication/

Johnson, Sharon .L. (2004) *Therapist's Guide to Clinical Intervention:* Academic Press

Kovanen, Mari (2017) *Building on your confidence: The personal bill of rights*
https://www.drmarikovanen.co.uk/building-confidence-personal-bill-rights/

Bourne, E. Ph.D (2015): *The Anxiety and Phobia Workbook:* New Harbinger

Unknown (Unknown) *Why Healthy Boundaries Are So Important in Recovery:* Ashley Addiction Treatment
https://www.ashleytreatment.org/boundaries-in-recovery/#:~:text=Internal%20boundaries%20are%20between%20you%20and%20you.&text=You%20might%20%20think%20of%20internal,commitments%20you%20make%20to%20yourself.

Cowan, Katy (2019) *How To Conquer Your Inner Demons And Be More Creative:* Creative Boom
https://www.creativeboom.com/tips/how-to-conquer-your-inner-demons-and-free-yourself-from-negativity/

BBC (2009) *The Four Noble Truths*: BBC
https://www.bbc.co.uk/religion/religions/buddhism/beliefs/fournobletruths_1.shtml

Townsend Williams, M. (2015) *Do Breathe: Calm Your Mind. Find Focus. Get Stuff Done*:
D Books

Akhtar, A & Ward, M. (2020) *25 people who became highly successful after age 40*: Insider
https://www.businessinsider.com/24-people-who-became-highly-successful-after-age-40-2015-6?r=US&IR=T#stan-lee-created-his-first-hit-comic-the-fantastic-four-just-shy-of-his-39th-birthday-in-1961-in-the-next-few-years-he-created-the-legend-ary-marvel-universe-whose-characters-such-as-spider-man-and-the-x-men-became-american-cultural-icons-1

Berry, Jennifer (2017) *What's to know about codependent relationships?* : Medical News
Today
https://www.medicalnewstoday.com/articles/319873#:~:text=Depend-ent%3A%20Two%20people%20rely%20on%20each%20other%20for%20support%20and%20love.&text=Dependent%3A%20Both%20people%20can%20ex-press,and%20will%20not%20express%20them.

Seltzer, L. F. (2014) *Codependent or Simply Dependent: What's the Big Difference?* Psychology
Today
https://www.psychologytoday.com/gb/blog/evolution-the-self/201412/codepend-ent-or-simply-dependent-what-s-the-big-difference

Ghannad, A (2016) *Leadership: The Journey Through Independence to Interdependence*:
The Ghannad Group
https://theghannadgroup.com/blog/leadership-interdependence

Enderwick, B.W (2019) *Saying You Are "Self-made" is Bullshit*: Medium
https://kaizenbarry.medium.com/saying-you-are-self-made-is-bullshit-f3922762c530

Blakey, Dr John (2012) *Codependent No More*: Challenging Coaching
https://challengingcoaching.co.uk/co-dependency-3/

Blakey, Dr John (2016) *Three simple and essential questions about how to win trust*: Chal-lenging Coaching
https://challengingcoaching.co.uk/three-simple-and-essential-questions-about-how-to-win-trust/

Bundrant, M (2018) *10 Signs You Have Trust Issues and How to Begin Healing*: Psych Central
https://psychcentral.com/blog/nlp/2016/11/trust-issues#_noHeaderPrefixedContent

Labossiere, S (2019) *3 Ways To Overcome Trust Issues* 30 Aug
https://www.youtube.com/watch?v=162q6hyBNes

Scott, E (Unknown) *The Power Of Leverage Will Make You Rich*: Street Directory https://www.streetdirec-tory.com/travel_guide/141509/how_to_grow_wealth/the_power_of_leverage_will_make_you_rich.html

The Intersteller New Deal (Unknown) *The 8 Philosophical Pillars For Peace Within Humanity*: The Interstellar New Deal https://interstellarnewdeal.global/main-book-text/ii-global-domestic-policies/philo-sophical-foundations-for-humanitys-transformation/the-7-philosophical-pillars-for-peace-within-humanity/

Gerber, Michael E (2001) *The E-Myth Revisted: Why Most Small Business Don't Work and What to Do About It*: HarperBus

Printed in Great Britain
by Amazon

79871284R00130